In the same series:

ANATOLIA I (From the beginnings to the end of the 2nd millennium B.C.)	U. Bahadır Alkım, Professor at the University of Istanbul
ANATOLIA II (From the 1st millennium B.C. to the end of the Roman period)	Henri Metzger, Professor at the University of Lyons
BYZANTIUM	Antoine Bon, Professor at the University of Lyons
CELTS AND GALLO-ROMANS	Jean-Jacques Hatt, Professor at the University of Strasbourg
CENTRAL AMERICA	Claude F. Baudez, Research Professor at the Centre National de la Recherche Scientifique (C.N.R.S.), Paris
CENTRAL ASIA	Aleksandr Belenitsky, Professor at the Archaeologi- cal Institute of Leningrad
CHINA	Vadime Elisseeff, Curator of the Cernuschi Museum, Paris
CRETE	Nicolas Platon, former Superintendent of Antiquities, Crete; former Director of the Acropolis Museum, Athens
CYPRUS	Vassos Karageorghis, Director of the Archaeological Museum, Nicosia
EGYPT	Jean Leclant, Professor at the Sorbonne, Paris
THE ETRUSCANS	Raymond Bloch, Professor at the Sorbonne, Paris
GREAT MORAVIA	Anton Točik, Director of the Archaeological Insti- tute of Nitra (Czechoslovakia)
GREECE I (Mycenaean and geometric periods)	Nicolas Platon, former Superintendent of Antiquities, Crete; former Director of the Acropolis Museum, Athens
GREECE II (Post-geometric periods)	François Salviat, Professor at the University of Aix- en-Provence
INDIA	Maurizio Taddei, Inspector of Oriental Art and Archaeology, Rome
INDOCHINA	Bernard P. Groslier, Curator of Historical Monu- ments, Angkor; Director of Archaeological Research at the Ecole Française d'Extrême-Orient

INDONESIA	Bernard P. Groslier, Curator of Historical Monuments, Angkor; Director of Archaeological Research at the Ecole Française d'Extrême-Orient
JAPAN	Vadime Elisseeff, Curator at the Cernuschi Museum, Paris
MESOPOTAMIA	Jean-Claude Margueron, Agrégé of the University, Paris; Member of the French Institute of Archaeology of Beirut
MEXICO	Jacques Soustelle
PERSIA I (From the origins to the Achaemenids)	Jean-Louis Huot, Agrégé of the University, Paris; Member of the French Institute of Archaeology of Beirut
PERSIA II (From the Seleucids to the Sassanids)	Vladimir Lukonin, Head of the Oriental Department, Hermitage Museum, Leningrad
PERU	† Rafael Larco Hoyle, Director of the Rafael Larco Herrera Museum, Lima
PREHISTORY	Denise de Sonneville-Bordes, Ph. D.
ROME	Gilbert Picard, Professor at the Sorbonne, Paris
RUMANIA	Constantin Daicoviciu, Director of the Archaeological Institute of Cluj, and Emil Condurachi, Director of the Archaeological Institute of Bucarest
SOUTHERN CAUCASUS	Boris B. Piotrovsky, Director of the Hermitage Museum, Leningrad
SOUTHERN SIBERIA	Mikhail Gryaznov, Professor at the Archaeological Institute, Leningrad
SYRIA-PALESTINE I (Ancient Orient)	Jean Perrot, Head of the French Archaeological Mission in Israel
SYRIA-PALESTINE II (Classical Orient)	Michael Avi Yonah, Professor at the University of Jerusalem and David Ussishkin from the University of Tel Aviv
THE TEUTONS	R. Hachmann, Professor at the University of Saarbrücken
TIBET	Giuseppe Tucci, President of the Italian Institute for the Middle and Far East, Rome
URARTU	Boris B. Piotrovsky, Director of the Hermitage Museum, Leningrad

ANCIENT CIVILIZATIONS

Series prepared under the direction of
Jean Marcadé, Professor of Archaeology
at the University of Bordeaux

RAFAEL LARCO HOYLE

PERU

Translated from the French by JAMES HOGARTH

91 illustrations in colour; 76 illustrations in black and white

 Barrie & Jenkins London

CONTENTS

PREFACE

The present volume stands a little apart in the series Archaeologia Mundi. *In saying this, I do not mean to imply that we had ever contemplated leaving the American continent out of our survey of modern archaeology in all its aspects; but, as the reader will see, this is a contribution to Peruvian archaeology rather than an introduction to the problems, the methods and the results of archaeological work in Peru.*

This difference of approach is not the responsibility of the author alone; but an initial misunderstanding has led to a most rewarding result. European students have long wished to have available in their own language, in a convenient form, the theories of a scholar who belongs to a famous family and is an accepted authority in America; and now we have them, expressed with all the spontaneity of a lecture delivered in the author's very personal style. For a long time, too, those concerned with this field, tantalised by the renown of a private collection known to contain such a prodigious wealth of material, have hankered after an opportunity to study a reasonable selection of this material; and now Don Rafael Larco Hoyle has made this possible by authorising M. Louis Nagel, during a recent visit to Peru, to photograph whatever unpublished material he thought necessary to accompany the text.

The reader who is not an expert in these matters will realise, therefore, that the illustrations in this book are not only of interest in themselves but are of considerable scientific value. And he must not be surprised if from time to time he finds a personal emphasis being put on certain points, detects a note of personal involvement, or finds himself being led into a discussion of technical details on certain questions on which, if I may adapt a phrase, archaeologi certant. *But I am sure that he will find the book all the more fascinating for the direct contact it gives him with the problems of archaeology in Peru.*

J. M.

I should like to express my gratitude to His Excellency Baron Jules de Koenigs-warter, Ambassador of France in Peru, Dr. Oscar Trelles, His Excellency Sr Alberto Wagner de Reyna, Secretary General in the Ministry of External Relations of Peru, Messrs. Jean Le Cannelier, Yoshito Amano, Raul Apesteguia and Mme Paul Fouchet for the invaluable help they have given in the preparation of this work.

INTRODUCTION

My interest in Peruvian archaeology began in 1924, stimulated by enthusiasm for the rich past of my native country, which my father had taught me to love; and it did not take me long to realise how inadequate our knowledge then was to provide a solid basis for the classification of the civilisations of Peru. It is true that we possessed the works which still form the foundation of studies in this field. The three great pioneers were Max Uhle, Julio C. Tello and Alfred Kroeber; but though their researches opened up much new ground they were not sufficient to reveal the cultural development of the patchwork of small peoples who lived in pre-Columbian Peru.

Thus when I began to write my book on the Mochicas I at once came up against gaps in archaeological knowledge which it was necessary to fill. I had, therefore, to set to work to establish the chronological order of the various stages of cultural development in Peru. The results of this work were published for the first time in my book, *Los Mochicas*, which appeared in 1938. By 1946 I had completed a table arranging the civilisations of northern Peru in chronological sequence, basing myself on discoveries made in the course of my own investigations. Then came a "round table" conference at Chiclín, which brought together, for the first time for many years, the best known archaeologists of North America (Dr. Alfred Kroeber and Dr. Mason unfortunately being unable to attend) and also some Peruvian archaeologists; and as a result the pattern of archaeological studies was completely renewed and a solid basis provided for future research. The North American archaeologists accepted the seven epochs into which I had divided the cultural sequence in Peru, sometimes changing the names but retaining the substance of what I had proposed.

In this system the cultural development of Peru is classified into seven epochs: the Pre-Ceramic Epoch, the Early Ceramic Epoch, the Epoch of Development or Formative Epoch, the Florescent Epoch, the Epoch of Fusion, the Imperial Epoch and the Epoch of the Conquest. Each of these epochs is in turn subdivided into three periods, so that the whole course of development of the different cultures can be set out in an orderly way. The epochs are of considerable length, and within the confines of each one different civilisations may grow up and decline and die. Within an epoch, too, there may be cultural phases which have not the status of independent civilisations but may serve to link one civilisation with another. Some subdivision is necessary, therefore, for the purposes of the chronological framework adopted in this book.

For archaeologists concerned with Peru the most useful working tool and diagnostic guide is the pottery. The first two epochs are defined by the absence of pottery and by its first beginnings. In the five following epochs – the epochs of formation, of culmination or florescence, of fusion, of the establishment of great kingdoms or empires, and finally of the destruction of the native civilisations – I have still used the pottery as the main identifying feature of each epoch, but I have named the epochs after the different stages of economic and political development of the peoples of Peru up to the arrival of the invaders who destroyed the native cultures.

These seven epochs, therefore, constitute the framework used in this book for the archaeological study of Peru and for the brief descriptions of the various civilisations which can be distinguished within the epochs. Some archaeologists, however, would like to return to the older classification, and – disregarding the real course of development of the various civilisations – would divide the cultural progression in Peru into an Initial Period, an Early Intermediate Period and a Late Intermediate Period. Although the names are changed, this is still the same basic classification as in the earliest days of Peruvian archaeology. Within these periods a number of "horizons" are recognised: an early horizon marked by what is called the Chavín culture, a middle horizon constituted by the Tiahuanaco or Huari culture, and a late horizon represented by the Inca dominance. I am firmly convinced that in archaeology it is wrong to reduce data of such importance to an oversimplified classification of this kind. We are concerned with the development of the civilisations of a whole complex of different peoples, and we must be sure that the classification we adopt fits in with the various stages of their development.

The division of Peruvian culture into an Initial, an Early Intermediate and a Late Intermediate Period may give some indication of the passage of time, but it tells us nothing of what happened during this time – of men's slow struggle to overcome their ignorance, of the flowering of their cultures, of the decadence that followed, of the great conquests which led to the formation of powerful kingdoms, and finally of the dominance of the vast Inca empire. The subdivision of this process cannot be merely a subdivision in time but must, at each stage, reflect the state of development of the different cultures.

But it is not merely this broad division into three periods that is open to objection. It is surely a retrograde step to disregard the latest scientific discoveries like radiocarbon dating and revert to the old system of horizons defined by reference

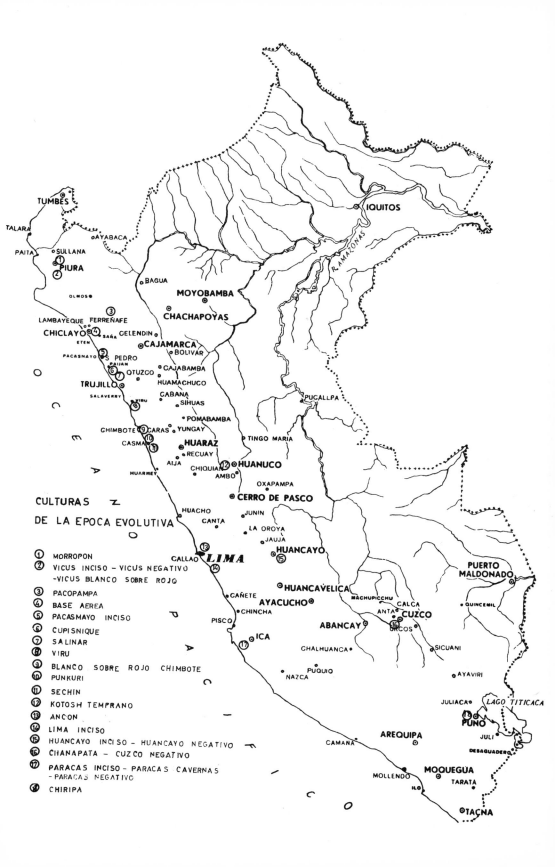

TUMBES

TALARA

PAITA   ○SULLANA
         ①PIURA
         ②

                ○AYABACA

        OLMOS○   ○BAGUA

                        MOYOBAMBA
                ③   CHACHAPOYAS
LAMBAYEQUE FERREÑAFE
CHICLAYO○④ ○SAÑA ○CELENDIN
        ETEN
PACASMAYO ⑤ S PEDRO   CAJAMARCA○
        PAIJAN   ○BOLIVAR
         ⑥⑦ OTUZCO   ○CAJABAMBA
TRUJILLO   HUAMACHUCO○
        SALAVERRY   CABANA○
         ⑧VIRU   SIHUAS
                      ○POMABAMBA
CHIMBOTE○⑨ CARAS ○YUNGAY
CASMA○ ⑩   ○TINGO MARIA
      ⑪ HUARAZ○
          ○RECUAY
        AIJA ⑫ HUANUCO
      HUARMEY CHIQUIAN○
              AMBO○
                  ○OXAPAMPA
CULTURAS   ○CERRO DE PASCO

DE LA EPOCA EVOLUTIVA
              HUACHO○ ○JUNIN
              CANTA○ ○LA OROYA
① MORROPON   ○JAUJA
② VICUS INCISO – VICUS NEGATIVO   ⑬ HUANCAYO○
   –VICUS BLANCO SOBRE ROJO   CALLAO LIMA ⑮
③ PACOPAMPA   ⑭
④ BASE AEREA   HUANCAVELICA○
⑤ PACASMAYO INCISO   ○CAÑETE
⑥ CUPISNIQUE   CHINCHA○ AYACUCHO○
⑦ SALINAR   PISCO○
⑧ VIRU   ○ICA
⑨ BLANCO SOBRE ROJO CHIMBOTE   ⑰
⑩ PUNKURI
⑪ SECHIN   ○PUQUIO
⑫ KOTOSH TEMPRANO   ○NAZCA
⑬ ANCON
⑭ LIMA INCISO
⑮ HUANCAYO INCISO – HUANCAYO NEGATIVO
⑯ CHANAPATA – CUZCO NEGATIVO
⑰ PARACAS INCISO – PARACAS CAVERNAS
   –PARACAS NEGATIVO
⑱ CHIRIPA

IQUITOS

R. AMAZONAS

PUCALLPA

PUERTO
MALDONADO

MACHUPICCHU   ○QUINCEMIL
ANTA○ CALCA
     CUZCO○
     ⑯
     URCOS
CHALHUANCA○   ○SICUANI
ABANCAY○

              ○AYAVIRI

JULIACA○   LAGO TITICACA
         ⑱
         PUNO
         JULI
DESAGUADERO○

AREQUIPA○
CAMANA○

              MOQUEGUA○
MOLLENDO○   TARATA○
    ILO○
              ○TACNA

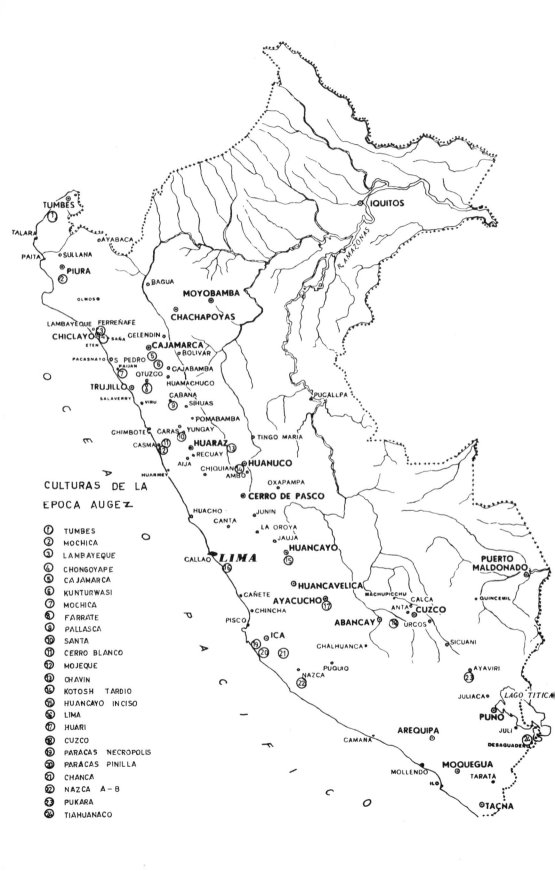

TUMBES
TALARA
PAITA
SULLANA
PIURA
OLMOS
BAGUA
IQUITOS
MOYOBAMBA
CHACHAPOYAS
LAMBAYEQUE FERREÑAFE
CHICLAYO
ETEN
SAÑA GELENDIN
CAJAMARCA
BOLIVAR
PACASMAYO
S PEDRO
PAIJAN
OTUZCO
CAJABAMBA
HUAMACHUCO
TRUJILLO
SALAVERRY
VIRU
CABANA
SIHUAS
POMABAMBA
CHIMBOTE
CARAS
YUNGAY
CASMA
HUARAZ
RECUAY
TINGO MARIA
AIJA
CHIQUIAN
HUANUCO
AMBO
HUARMEY
OXAPAMPA
CERRO DE PASCO
HUACHO
JUNIN
CANTA
LA OROYA
JAUJA
CALLAO
LIMA
HUANCAYO
PUERTO MALDONADO
HUANCAVELICA
QUINCEMIL
CAÑETE
AYACUCHO
MACHUPICCHU
CALCA
CHINCHA
ANTA
CUZCO
PISCO
ABANCAY
URCOS
ICA
CHALHUANCA
SICUANI
NAZCA
PUQUIO
AYAVIRI
JULIACA
LAGO TITICACA
PUNO
JULI
AREQUIPA
CAMANA
DESAGUADERO
MOQUEGUA
MOLLENDO
TARATA
ILO
TACNA

R. AMAZONAS
PUCALLPA
AYABACA

CULTURAS DE LA EPOCA AUGE

1. TUMBES
2. MOCHICA
3. LAMBAYEQUE
4. CHONGOYAPE
5. CAJAMARCA
6. KUNTURWASI
7. MOCHICA
8. FARRATE
9. PALLASCA
10. SANTA
11. CERRO BLANCO
12. MOJEQUE
13. CHAVIN
14. KOTOSH TARDIO
15. HUANCAYO INCISO
16. LIMA
17. HUARI
18. CUZCO
19. PARACAS NECROPOLIS
20. PARACAS PINILLA
21. CHANCA
22. NAZCA A-B
23. PUKARA
24. TIAHUANACO

P A C I F I C O

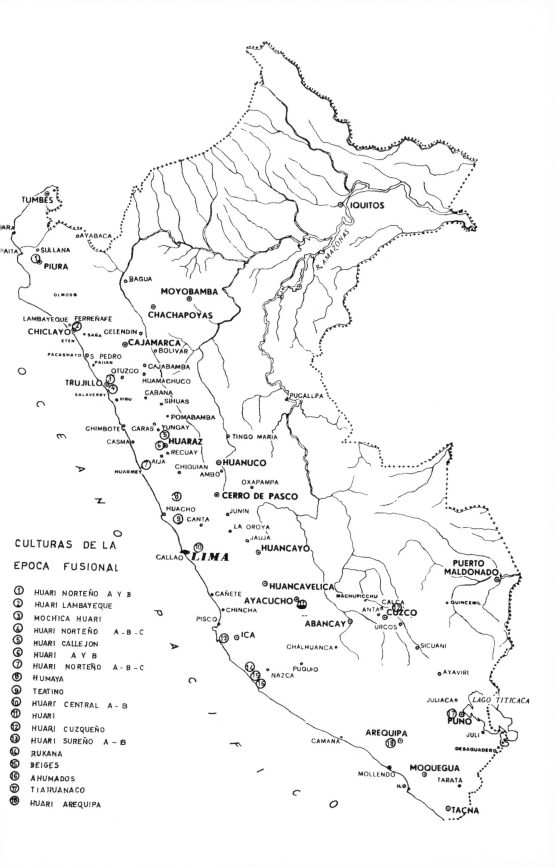

TUMBES

IQUITOS

AYABACA

SULLANA
① PIURA

BAGUA

MOYOBAMBA

OLMOS

CHACHAPOYAS

LAMBAYEQUE FERREÑAFE
CHICLAYO ②
ETEN SAÑA GELENDIN
PACASMAYO S PEDRO CAJAMARCA
PAIJAN BOLIVAR
QTUZCO CAJABAMBA
③ HUAMACHUCO
TRUJILLO ④ CABANA
SALAVERRY SIHUAS
VIRU

PUCALLPA

POMABAMBA
CHIMBOTE CARAS YUNGAY
CASMA ⑤ HUARAZ
⑥ RECUAY
⑦ AIJA CHIQUIAN TINGO MARIA
HUARMEY AMBO HUANUCO

OXAPAMPA
⑲ CERRO DE PASCO
HUACHO JUNIN
⑨ CANTA
LA OROYA
JAUJA
⑩ HUANCAYO
CALLAO LIMA

PUERTO
MALDONADO

HUANCAVELICA
CAÑETE MACHUPICCHU CALCA
CHINCHA AYACUCHO ⑪ ANTA CUZCO
PISCO ABANCAY URCOS
⑬ ICA QUINCEMIL

CHALHUANCA SICUANI
⑭ PUQUIO
⑮ NAZCA AYAVIRI
⑯

JULIACA LAGO TITICACA
⑰ PUNO
AREQUIPA JULI
⑱ DESAGUADERO

CAMANA

MOQUEGUA
MOLLENDO TARATA
ILO

TACNA

R AMAZONAS

CULTURAS DE LA

EPOCA FUSIONAL

① HUARI NORTEÑO A Y B
② HUARI LAMBAYEQUE
③ MOCHICA HUARI
④ HUARI NORTEÑO   A - B - C
⑤ HUARI CALLEJON
⑥ HUARI   A Y B
⑦ HUARI NORTEÑO A - B - C
⑧ HUMAYA
⑨ TEATINO
⑩ HUARI CENTRAL A - B
⑪ HUARI
⑫ HUARI CUZQUEÑO
⑬ HUARI SUREÑO A - B
⑭ RUKANA
⑮ BEIGES
⑯ AHUMADOS
⑰ TIAHUANACO
⑱ HUARI AREQUIPA

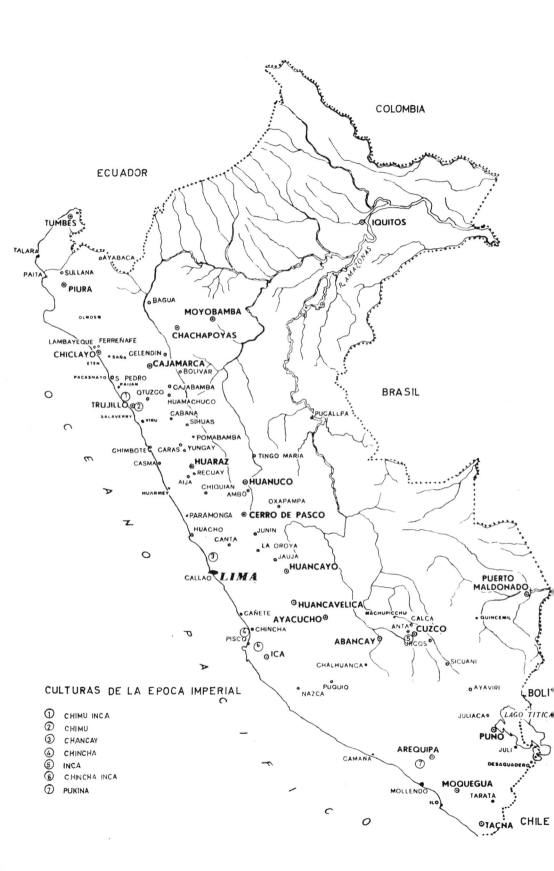

COLOMBIA

ECUADOR

TUMBES

TALARA

PAITA

SULLANA

PIURA

OLMOS

BAGUA

MOYOBAMBA

CHACHAPOYAS

LAMBAYEQUE FERREÑAFE

CHICLAYO

SAÑA CELENDIN

ETEN

PACASMAYO S PEDRO

CAJAMARCA

BOLIVAR

PAIJAN

OTUZCO

CAJABAMBA

TRUJILLO ①②

HUAMACHUCO

SALAVERRY

VIRU

CABANA

SIHUAS

POMABAMBA

CHIMBOTE CARAS YUNGAY

CASMA

HUARAZ

TINGO MARIA

RECUAY

AIJA

CHIQUIAN

HUANUCO

HUARMEY

AMBO

OXAPAMPA

PARAMONGA

CERRO DE PASCO

HUACHO

JUNIN

CANTA

LA OROYA

③

JAUJA

CALLAO

LIMA

HUANCAYO

HUANCAVELICA

CAÑETE

AYACUCHO

MACHUPICCHU

CALCA

CHINCHA

ANTA

CUZCO

QUINCEMIL

PISCO ④

⑤

URCOS

ABANCAY

SICUANI

ICA ⑤

CHALHUANCA

IQUITOS

R. AMAZONAS

BRASIL

PUCALLPA

PUERTO MALDONADO

NAZCA

PUQUIO

AYAVIRI

BOLI

JULIACA

LAGO TITICA

PUNO

JULI

DESAGUADERO

CULTURAS DE LA EPOCA IMPERIAL

① CHIMU INCA
② CHIMU
③ CHANCAY
④ CHINCHA
⑤ INCA
⑥ CHINCHA INCA
⑦ PUKINA

AREQUIPA

⑦

CAMANA

MOQUEGUA

MOLLENDO

TARATA

ILO

TACNA CHILE

to refuse deposits and the relative levels of tombs, which were thought in their day to provide reasonably satisfactory chronological landmarks. The Peruvian "horizons" are an illusion. The cultures, pseudo-cultures and decorative styles which are given the name of horizons are nothing of the kind. This is because their development is irregular; and moreover, we find that in certain places a style persists, continuing from one epoch to another, or from one period to another within an epoch, in a way incompatible with the idea of a horizon.

In other areas cultures have a long period of development and then expansion. Thus the Huari civilisation and the Inca culture itself developed at Ayacucho and Cuzco, reaching their apogee in the Florescent Epoch, after some fifteen hundred years; then eight hundred years later, at the end of the Florescent Epoch, we find the Huari civilisation extending over Peru. We do not know how long it took the Huari people to conquer the whole country, though it must have required many centuries; but if we take only the period from the beginning of the Florescent Epoch to the beginning of the Epoch of Fusion there is still a lapse of eight hundred years. The Huari civilisation cannot, therefore, be regarded as a horizon. Similarly with the Incas. There are jars of Inca form with Huari motifs. At the time when Huari dominated the Collao area, about 1400 A.D., Inca armies arrived in the north of Peru; but a very long period of time must have elapsed between the formation of the Inca culture in the mountains of Cuzco and the achievement of Inca dominance over the whole of Peru.

In some cases, too, we find these cultures and pseudo-cultures surviving much longer in some areas than in others. Thus some of the cultures of the Formative Epoch continue to develop, retaining the characteristic features of this epoch, and reach their culmination in the Florescent Epoch; others, after reaching their peak in this epoch, continue into the Epoch of Fusion and then expand throughout Peru.

The "early horizon" is thought of as including the civilisations of Chavín, Paracas and Cupisnique among others. In the Chavín culture are included a series of local cultures found throughout Peru, characterised by pottery fired in closed kilns, blackish-brown in colour and with incised decoration. The motifs are frequently geometric – representations of leaves and flowers, for example – but tend mainly to be of religious significance, representing the feline god, or some part of it, or minor deities. We also find a series of jars painted by the application of a black slip.

The excavations at Vicus, Chongoyape and other sites in the Department of Lambayeque, the discoveries I made at Cupisnique, and the finds at Virú, Casma, Nepeña, Ancón, Cotosh, Paracas and elsewhere in Peru make it quite clear that even in pottery belonging to the same period there are distinct differences in the forms, the decorative motifs and the modelling.

The cultures of the middle period of the Formative Epoch are characterised by incised ornament, for the men of this period had not yet discovered the technique of positive painting. Nor at this stage do we find any gold, for metals were not yet known. As an expression of the religious beliefs of these peoples we find only the feline god rearing on his hind legs, in a first attempt at anthropomorphism. The artists display a lively imagination: the tendency towards the stylised representation of the god has begun, but the excavations at Chiclayo, Cupisnique, Cotosh and elsewhere show that the incised decoration which characterises the pottery of the middle period of the Formative Epoch went through a number of different stages. I defined these stages – from the Pre-Cupisnique to the Cupisnique of Santa Ana and, in the Florescent Epoch, the Chavín temple and Cerro Blanco – in my book *Los Cupisniques*, and subsequent excavations have confirmed my views.

At Chongoyape objects in wrought gold were found alongside pottery with incised decoration; and the same type of pottery, though more refined than at Cupisnique, was found on the Hacienda Fárrate near Sallapullo in the valley of the Rio Chicama along with fine gold plaques with repoussé representations of the three deities.

In the Nepeña valley we find two stages represented by the temples of Punkurí and Cerro Blanco. At Paracas there are three stages – Cavernas, Necrópolis and Pinilla. All these tombs contain gold objects, and Paracas Necrópolis is also notable for its magnificent textiles. They must be assigned to the Florescent Epoch. Finally the Chavín temple, the finest achievement of the style which developed during the Formative Epoch, is contemporary with the Mochica III culture, whose pottery shows the typical banded reliefs characteristic of the decoration of this great temple, perhaps the finest of Peruvian antiquity. It is clear, therefore, that Peru possessed an artistic tradition which was no less enduring than the great styles developed in other parts of the world. When the Sechín and Cupisnique reliefs and the pottery from tombs belonging to the early period of the Formative Epoch are compared with the splendid bas-reliefs in the Chavín temple it does not take an expert to see that the Chavín reliefs belong to a very advanced stage of artistic development, a period of cultural flowering. The Chavín style, indeed, shows such a riot of flamboyant ornament that it has at times a rather decadent effect.

It is thus an error to say that merely because we find particular patterns, incised or in relief, on certain buildings, monoliths or other objects these things therefore belong to a particular period of time.

In the Formative Epoch we find three decorative styles, the three basic styles of Peruvian pottery. Alongside these styles the shapes of pottery and the techniques of architecture arise and develop. We see the beginnings of metal-working, and of the different techniques and distinctive features of textile production. These three pan-Peruvian decorative styles can be followed from the beginning and throughout the development of the cultures which were to reach their full flowering in the Florescent Epoch.

As noted above, the value of radiocarbon dating has been disputed because it gave different dates for the same culture. Yet it is surely reasonable to find varying dates since, as I have shown, there are some cultures and styles which continued in existence longer on some sites than on others. Thus we sometimes find cultures or styles continuing from the Formative Epoch into the Florescent Epoch, or from this epoch into the Epoch of Fusion. The Cupisnique tombs, which yielded pottery of the style known as "classic Chavín", cannot possibly be assigned the same date as a tomb at Chongoyape or the Chavín temple, where incised pottery was also found. Similarly the pottery of Vicus, of Virú and of Santa cannot be of the same date as the Recuay vases, which are associated with pottery decorated in the negative painting technique; nor can the negative-painted pottery of Paracas. Similarly also with the type of pottery known as Huari, sometimes called Tiahuanaco or Tiahuanacoid. This is found in three different phases, beginning with the time when, as noted above, the Huari culture spread throughout the whole of Peru; and these three Huari types, which I have designated A, B and C, cannot be assigned to the same period as the typical pottery found in the excavations at Huari itself and on other neighbouring sites.

It was reasonable enough for Wendell Bennett to talk of the "white-on-red" and the "negative" horizon, for he regarded them as horizons and not as decorative styles. At that time, however, the different types of negative-painted pottery had not yet been discovered, apart from the specimens which I was able to show him in the Rafael Larco Herrera Museum. But to seek to depreciate the fundamental importance of the style of negative decoration and the white-on-red style is tantamount to a refusal to follow the course of Peruvian decorative art from its beginnings and throughout its later development.

Nor is it correct to say, as a well known archaeologist has done, that the Chavín culture is the mother of the later civilisations of Peru. If this were so we should now have to speak of a number of pseudo-cultures; for it was the techniques and styles developed during the Formative Epoch which gave rise in the Florescent Epoch to the cultures which are marked by clearly defined and unmistakeable characteristics of their own, and can therefore be classed with certainty as distinct and separate cultures.

Wendell Bennett used frequently to discuss with me the three horizons which he called Chavín, negative and white-on-red. If, however, we are to consider the Chavín culture as a horizon because its pottery has incised decoration and its people worshipped the stylised feline of the Formative Epoch, then equally we are entitled to give the name of horizon or of culture to any context in which we find negative decoration or white-on-red. It is true that the latest discoveries have revealed additional sites yielding incised pottery similar to that of Cupisnique; but other excavations have given us more sites with negative-decorated or white-on-red pottery. When those who maintain that Chavín is a culture have it demonstrated to them that the incised pottery of Paracas Cavernas is quite different from Cupisnique pottery, and that there are differences between the corresponding pottery at Ancón and Virú and the incised pottery of Morropón, they suggest that these are merely local variations. It is difficult to maintain this argument: these are not merely local variations, they are distinct cultures of the Formative Epoch in which we can discern the first intimations of the principal civilisation of the Florescent Epoch. If incised decoration is found on all the pottery this is simply because at this stage the techniques of positive and negative painting had not yet been discovered.

During the transitional phase colour was applied only within the areas marked out by incised lines: we find examples of this at Cupisnique, Paracas Cavernas, Chongoyape, Morropón and Vicus. Nor is it surprising to find also the stylised feline rearing on its hind legs in the "rampant" position. At this period the Peruvian peoples were still at a relatively early stage of spiritual development, and throughout the whole country the feline was the principal deity who, with his attendant minor deities, ruled over the supernatural world.

1

2

3

4

5

6

11

12

13, 14, 15, 16, 17, 18, 19, 20, 21 →

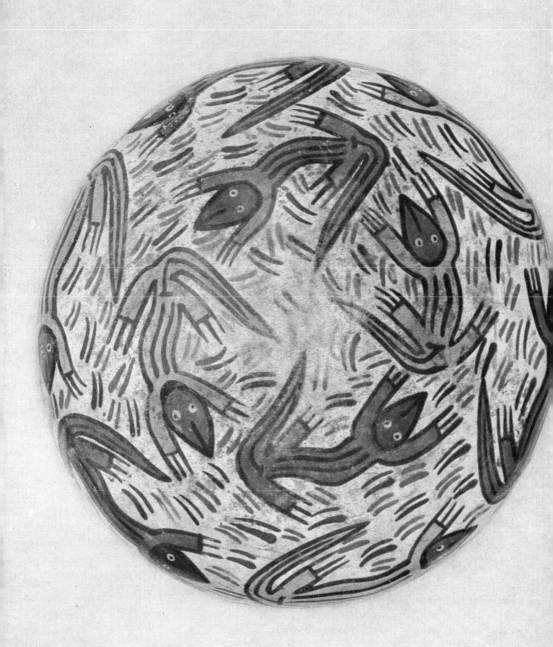

If we give the name of Chavin culture to the culture characterised by pottery with incised decoration we are no less entitled to distinguish a culture marked by pottery with negative decoration. Jars with this type of decoration have been found at Tumbes, Vicus, Lambayeque, La Libertad, Virú, Santa, Nepeña, Callejón de Huaylas, Lima, Paracas, Arequipa, Cuzco and Puno, and here we make the same observation as with the incised jars of the Formative Epoch: the pottery from these various sites is differentiated, but nevertheless shows features which contribute to the development of the cultures of the Florescent Epoch. The feline found in these areas is the same: not yet anthropomorphic in form but showing the beginnings of stylisation.

We must now consider the pottery with white painting on a red base, which is of no less importance. It is found, showing the same influences, at Vicus, La Libertad, Santa, Callejón de Huaylas, Lima, Paracas and elsewhere. As with the negative-decorated jars, the white-on-red pottery of Vicus cannot stand comparison with the similar pottery from the Chicama valley; and this in turn cannot be compared with the pottery of Lima, still less with that of Nazca. Clearly these are pan-Peruvian decorative styles which were found throughout the country and were used by the cultures which were in process of development during the Formative Epoch. It is quite wrong, therefore, to pick out one, two or three common features and on their account to define as a "culture" a whole series of peoples with other features which are entirely distinct.

Incised decoration is not peculiar to Peru. It is found also in Ecuador, Colombia, Mexico, the United States and Africa; and indeed some African jars with incised decoration, a thick stirrup spout and a large neck are very like those found at Cupisnique. This does not, of course, entitle us to claim that all this pottery belongs to the same culture. The same is true of the negative decoration which is so common among many different peoples in America. To suppose that all this negative-decorated pottery belonged to a single culture, in the same way as the incised pottery, and that the white-on-red pottery belonged to a different culture, would plunge us into an abyss of error.

It follows from what has been said, therefore, that if Chavín is a culture there must have been two other pan-Peruvian cultures during the Formative Epoch, the culture of the negative-decorated pottery and the white-on-red culture. But this is not accepted by contemporary archaeologists, who seek to modify the chronological classification of cultures. In their view neither the negative-decorated jars nor the white-on-red jars represent a culture, or for that matter a horizon, although both types are found throughout Peru. But archaeology, like law, knows no exceptions: what applies to the pottery with incised decoration must apply also to the negative decoration and the white-on-red decoration of the pottery of the two other stages of the Formative Epoch. The three styles all contribute something to the crystallisation of the styles which differentiate the great cultures of the Florescent Epoch, the classic period in the cultural development of Peru.

It is interesting to note that negative decoration disappears from some areas but continues in others – for example in the Chicama valley, where we find Mochica jars with this type of decoration. In other regions again it flourishes in its purest form: for example at Virú and at Santa, where it puts its special stamp on the formation of the Santa culture (Callejón de Huaylas). In other words, its development is identical with that of the cultures which produced pottery with incised decoration. Later it was the white-on-red style which stimulated the development of the technique of positive painting which lasted until the end of the native cultures. It would therefore be flying in the face of the facts to disregard these two great pan-Peruvian styles; and indeed the study of these styles suggests conclusions of the greatest importance to Peruvian archaeology. The three decorative styles we have been discussing, along with the other discoveries which accompanied them, provided the basis for the development of the great cultures which crystallised and reached their peak in the classical period of Peru, forming a splendid complex of civilisations which can stand comparison with the civilisations of Mexico and of Mesopotamia.

And finally, if the Chavín culture were accepted as constituting the Chavín horizon, because its pottery has incised decoration and thick stirrup spouts, we should then have to regard the pan-Peruvian Chavín pseudo-culture as a pan-American culture. This conclusion would follow because incised jars like those called Chavín are found in Ecuador, Colombia, Mexico, the United States, Bolivia and elsewhere. And by the same token it would be necessary to regard as pan-Peruvian and pan-American the cultures of all the peoples with negative-decorated or white-on-red pottery.

For the reasons we have been considering, therefore, it is important not to confuse a generalised decorative style with a "culture" or a "horizon", particularly during the formative stage of a civilisation. At this period we see the beginnings of incised and relief decoration; then comes the fleeting appearance of negative decoration; then we have the first jars with positive decoration, simple and spontaneous in style, giving a foretaste of the skill in painting which distinguished native Peruvian art and which – along with the later development of sculptural modelling – was to give Peru its particular place in the history of the ancient art of America.

The more we study these early stages of art in America, the more likely it seems that these three styles, which formed the basis of the art of pottery painting in Peru, are not merely pan-Peruvian styles as we have shown them to be, but can now be regarded as pan-American.

My studies of the religion of the Mayas and of the Mochicas suggest that the religious ideas of these two peoples had much in common. The feline god, who formed the centre of the spiritual world of the Peruvians, was also the principal figure in the beliefs of the Mayas, whose main area of settlement extended from Yucatán to Guatemala. This in itself is not, however, a sufficient basis for postulating connections between the two peoples.

The Mochica script which I discovered is similar to Maya writing, and it is, therefore, possible to assert that the hieroglyphics which we find in the manuscripts or carved on stelae are representations of the Lima bean *(Phaseolus lunatus)* transformed by the Mayas into a hieroglyph. We must look for more connections of this kind, for they demonstrate a unity of belief, a unity of religious conceptions and of the deities worshipped. Their modes of writing are clear proof of a close link between the Mayas and the Peruvians, for the two scripts evidently have a common origin, being the only two writing systems in the world which enclose their characters in a cartouche.

The Olmec jade statuettes show the development of the feline which later became an anthropomorphic feline deity like the jaguar in Peru. We can watch this divine figure slowly evolving from the early period of the Formative Epoch and throughout the Florescent Epoch until it finally becomes Aia Paec, the anthropomorphic deity of the Mochicas and of the Peruvian people as a whole.

Basing myself on the similarity of the Maya and Peruvian scripts, I have, since my first books, pointed to the existence of these connections between the two peoples. We must still, however, confine ourselves to noting that the connections did exist, for we cannot yet demonstrate the origin of the common elements in the two cultures or say when the exchanges between them took place.

In this preface I have tried to summarise some contemporary approaches to the classification of the cultures of Peru, in preparation for the analysis, on which we must now embark, of the various epochs and of the cultures which flourished at different epochs and in different periods of these epochs. It must, of course, be recognised that there are still gaps in our knowledge – particularly from the Early Ceramic Epoch to the Formative Epoch – which make it impossible to give a complete and logical account of the civilisations of Peru. Recent discoveries have thrown much fresh light on the archaeology of Peru, and I am convinced that a little further work, methodically conducted, could – particularly in northern Peru – add considerably to our knowledge and fill in the remaining gaps.

There is room also for further study of the cultural influences which have come from outside Peru; and conversely we are still uncertain of the period at which certain American peoples came under the influence of the civilisations of Peru. Careful and meticulous investigation is required in this field. We cannot claim to establish a connection between Peru and Mexico or some other country merely because we find in both countries a similar decorative technique or similar motifs like the Greek key or volutes or concentric circles; for styles or motifs may be developed in different ways in different parts of the world, without any link between the peoples concerned. Nor does it follow, when we find two peoples using the fish-hook or the needle or some other implement, or producing the same type of pottery, that there has been any connection between them. To reach conclusions in this field we must not only undertake thorough archaeological investigation of the material remains, but must also seek to understand the spiritual and intellectual world of the peoples concerned. Only in this way may we hope to acquire some insight into the mysteries of their past, which otherwise must remain closed to us.

THE PRE-CERAMIC EPOCH

I

Max Uhle, the eminent German archaeologist and a pioneer of Peruvian archaeology, maintained that advanced civilisations like those of the Mochica and Nazca peoples had a central American origin. In this he was in error, but this great scholar is nevertheless entitled to the credit of having laid the foundations of all later studies of pan-Peruvian culture. Dr. Julio C. Tello, that indefatigable investigator of Peruvian antiquities, found a stratum of incised pottery with representations of religious subjects and sculptured stones showing a feline erect on its hind legs; and on the basis of these finds he developed his theory of a Megalithic empire of Chavín earlier than the civilisations of the Florescent Epoch, modifying previous stratigraphic studies and adding to them the stage he called Chavín and regarded as the mother of all Peruvian civilisations. I myself was the first to express disagreement and state objections to this theory, although for Uhle himself I still feel profound admiration and respect; for in my excavations I had found poorly-fired red pottery at a lower level than Chavín.

My American colleagues who took part in the Virú expedition – the largest and best organised archaeological expedition ever to come to Peru – also found this pottery and called it Early Guañape. I had previously also discovered the pottery of Queneto, in tombs lying within large enclosures formed by lines of standing stones and ancient menhirs similar to the oldest structures found in the Old World. This discovery of the coarse pottery of Queneto in association with a type of structure which is considered the oldest in the world is an undisputed fact, and no one has been able to show that the date I assigned to this pottery immediately on its discovery was wrong. These finds completely changed our concept of the phase preceding the one to which Dr. Tello had given the name Chavín, and also made it necessary to modify his theory that the Chavín empire had been the origin of all Peruvian civilisations.

The eminent archaeologist Dr. Junius Bird, who came to Peru with the Virú expedition, was the first to make a proper study of pre-ceramic sites in Chile; and his discoveries at Huaca Prieta and at Cerro Prieto in the Virú valley demonstrated the existence of the Pre-Ceramic Epoch in Peru. Later he found javelin points in the Pampa de San Pedro, and I myself was fortunate enough to find some of these in the Pampa de Paiján and the Pampa de los Fósiles, where previously I had found thousands of fragments of pottery of the Cupisnique type which Tello assigned to Chavín. *(Plate 1)*

At Huaca Prieta no lance points or bones of land animals were found: only the bones of sea-lions, porpoises and sea birds. The occupants of this site seem to have lived mainly on fish.

Bird believes that a rudimentary form of agriculture existed at this period, although the population also depended largely on crabs, sea urchins, fish, starfish, clams and other shellfish. Their staple diet was made up of roots, small tubers and a few fruits found locally. Other plants found were lentils, red peppers, canna, tomatoes, the zapote or marmalade plum, and cotton (the 26-chromosome variety). There were also two types of squashes, of which the bottle gourd, *Lagenaria siceraria*, was the most frequently found: it was used not only as a food but as the raw material for making various vessels and floats for fishing. Cooking was done with hot stones, and a considerable number of stones have been found which had served this purpose. The occupants of the site lived in small huts, single-roomed dwellings with walls lined with pebbles. No sign of any religious beliefs has been found; their tombs were simple pits of irregular shape. They do not seem to have known the use of bead necklaces. Their textiles, splendidly patterned, are the oldest examples of decorative art in Peru, dating as they do from 2500 B.C., and their decorated gourds are impressive specimens of an art which had already developed well beyond the primitive stage.

At this period cotton was used for weaving, employing the simple technique known as twining. A few fragments have also been found showing the beginnings of real weaving, though still with a fairly primitive technique. Later, as reported in the *Bulletin* of the Rafael Larco Herrera Museum, published at Chiclín, I discovered Pre-Ceramic implements in the Paracas peninsula.

Thus the first progress was made in the discovery of the Pre-Ceramic stage in Peru, leading to the first division between hunters and fishermen – the hunters representing an earlier phase than the fishermen.

A little later I discovered in the Pampa de Paiján and the Pampa de los Fósiles the first shelters built of stones laid to form semicircular walls 35 to 45 feet long designed to provide protection from the wind. Within one of these shelters I found stone points and flakes. I also found what I believe to be the first temple, constructed from large stones, with a small wing projecting on each side to form a semicircular structure like that just described.

If I do not divide the earliest periods of Peruvian culture into a pre-agricultural and an agricultural stage, and prefer instead the terms Pre-Ceramic and Early Ceramic, this is because it seems to me relatively easy to determine, from the fragments of terracotta ware that have been found, the time at which pottery first appears; but it is not possible to say with equal certainty when men began to sow and to cultivate plants to meet their needs.

A number of later excavations have thrown further light on this period. From the discoveries at Lauricocha, with the help of radiocarbon dating, we know that the human remains in the Huánuco caves are roughly 10,000 years old. The stone implements found at Lauricocha are similar, though not identical, to those found in the Pampa de San Pedro and the Pampa de los Fósiles, and show a related technique. Some of the tools are worn, others have been re-shaped; and we find the same thing with the scrapers and knives. The javelin points from Lauricocha have a semicircular base; those found in the north have a small lug to give them a firmer grip. In addition to these stone objects the Lauricocha excavations also yielded pointed instruments made from the horns of the tarugo (the roe-deer of the high plateau). Clearly the men of this region, like those of the north, depended on hunting for their food, which consisted mainly of llama, guanaco and vicuña meat and, in the coastal area, of roe-deer.

It was during these 8,000 years of the Pre-Ceramic Epoch that men made new discoveries and innovations in agriculture, learning by experience to use plants for food, for making cloth from which they fashioned garments to protect them from the inclemencies of the weather, and for making nets for their fishing.

Junius Bird used radiocarbon dating on the organic material, obtaining an age of 2,600 years. Accordingly I would date Huaca Prieta in the middle and late periods of the Pre-Ceramic Epoch. The age accepted by Bird for the Pre-Ceramic is from 4,320 to 4,528 years, plus or minus, giving dates from 2370 to 2578 B.C.

Later, in the Paracas area, Frédéric Engel found human remains 5,000 years old at Cabeza Larga. Engel considers that these men practised a primitive form of agriculture, cultivating gourds and beans. In reality most of the people of this period lived by food-gathering: I do not believe that there existed any effective agriculture as a means of food production. The hunters obtained food by hunting the animals of the area where they lived. The fishermen gathered shellfish and probably hunted the sea-lion. Such was the way of life in the final period of the Pre-Ceramic Epoch.

Rushes were used to make clothes and to serve other domestic purposes, in a series of experiments which led at a later stage to the discovery of the weaving loom. By the end of this period the pattern of settlement was already beginning to alter, and small clusters of dwellings were being formed, like the beginnings of villages. It is noteworthy that the middens of Huaca Prieta required a trench 60 feet deep to reach the lowest strata: clearly it must have taken many years and a large number of people to produce such considerable mass of refuse.

At Toquepala decoration belonging to a less primitive stage was found on walls revealed in the excavations; and similar discoveries were made at Ancón, Asía and Chivateros. But although the Pre-Ceramic Epoch covered a considerable length of time, finds belonging to this epoch are relatively rare. Further and more exhaustive studies are required, therefore, before a definitive classification of the epoch can be established. At present it is dated to between 8,000 and 2,000 years before our era, but I have not the slightest doubt that further discoveries will soon be made going back to an earlier date than Lauricocha.

23

24

25

26

27

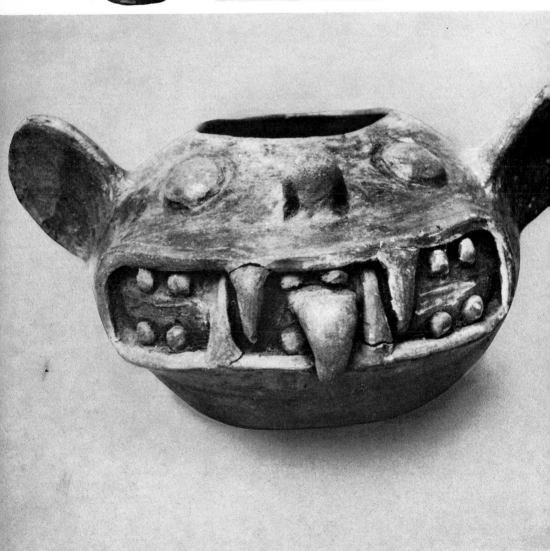

28

29

THE EARLY CERAMIC EPOCH

At San Ildefonso in the Virú valley, in the Department of La Libertad, just where the valley divides, and to the left of the Aguas Arriba valley, are the ruins of Queneto. Their form of construction makes them unique in Peru: within rectangular areas marked out by alignments of large stone slabs we find a number of menhirs, huge blocks of stone which have clearly been roughly squared. Similar buildings are found at Tiahuanaco, there they are known by the name of "Kalasasaya", a word which in the Aymara language means standing stone. But the resemblance is confined to the fact that in both places the walls mark out rectangular areas. The "Kalasasaya" of Tiahuanaco consists of a series of large stones standing at intervals in a straight line, with smaller stones filling in the gaps to form walls: at Queneto, on the other hand, the wall is built of large stones with a more or less flat surface standing close together.

Within one of these small enclosures at Queneto we found nine tombs containing bodies with funerary offerings of small terracotta vessels in the shape of gourds. Their thick walls show that the material had not been properly selected and that there was a good deal of sand in the mixture; some of them, indeed, seem to have been made of ordinary earth. These are not finds made in a single tomb but in a whole series of tombs, all with the same type of offerings. The fact that we find this crude pottery – made of unsuitable material, poorly fired and unpolished – in structures of the oldest type seems to me to show that we are concerned here with the very beginnings of pottery or with the very earliest stages of its development.

Alongside these tombs we find many stones bearing petroglyphs with designs of authentically primitive type. Similar petroglyphs have been found scattered throughout Peru. But we also find some belonging to the middle period of the Formative Epoch, which show considerable progress and are very different from those found at Queneto. This epoch saw the beginning of the cult of the menhirs, as well as the cult of the dead, and the use of terracotta jars as offerings to accompany the dead. In one of the petroglyphs we can distinguish a representation of a feline along with anthropomorphic figures. Man was already beginning to consider the feline as a being of importance, and it seems quite likely that the cult of this animal as a divinity began at this period.

In the course of our excavations in the Chicama and Santa Catalina valleys a similar type of pottery came to light; and some of this pottery has also been found in the deepest levels in other parts of Peru.

As time went on, man conceived the idea of decorating his pottery. He did this in the first place by applying knobs to the surface of his pots. Later came the first modelled pottery: rudimentary works which belong to the very infancy of art. They show something of the creative spirit of children – perhaps not even this, for the form of the animals represented is barely suggested. *(Plate 2)*

Finally, Edward Lanning contributed to our knowledge of the early phase of pottery by his discoveries in the Paita peninsula, on the south coast and at Ancón. José Matos found this phase at Ancón, as Engel did at Paracas. This stratum of pottery is earlier than the incised pottery called Chavín, to which I give the name Cupisnique, in the Chicama valley. This pottery is found throughout Peru, and where we find it we see the first steps of a civilisation in the process of formation.

The new discoveries confirm what I established – for the first time in the history of Peruvian archaeological studies – in the first volume of my book, *Los Mochicas*.

My examination of these remains had at first suggested that it was in the final period of this epoch that the use of moulds must have begun. I came to the conclusion, however, that pottery was still made by hand in the early years of the Formative Epoch, and that moulds were not manufactured and used until later. Clearly at the period with which we are concerned the art of pottery had come into existence. Man now had new resources available to him, and could begin to spell out the beauty which the art of modelling could make manifest. He now began the cult of the dead, making his funerary offerings to them; for clearly he was perplexed by the mystery of death. Already his thoughts were turned towards the after-life, which stimulated his faculties and inspired him to the quest of an immortal destiny.

THE FORMATIVE EPOCH

III

The Formative or Developmental Epoch is perhaps the most interesting, if not the most important, of the periods of Peruvian cultural development. As we follow the evolution of Peruvian culture through the centuries, this period is like a great crucible in which the various cultures which grew up on Peruvian soil were moulded in all their richness and diversity. It was during this period that the different civilisations first acquired their primary characteristics, determining the form in which they later crystallised. It was a period of invention and discovery, which saw the triumphant emergence of pottery in all its various forms and purposes; but not of pottery alone. Metal-working now appeared, and architecture achieved increased mastery. The art of weaving was perfected; new techniques were acquired and new implements invented. The patterns of civilisation began to take shape, so that in the Florescent Epoch the different cultures could achieve a rapid flowering, each with the specific characteristics which had been forged in the Formative Epoch.

It was the Formative Epoch that saw the beginnings of large-scale agriculture and the development of the valleys. Without proper drainage these became swamps which offered little scope for the cultivation of useful crops. At this period men set out to conquer the valleys, installing drainage channels to make the land cultivable, beginning upstream and working their way down gradually towards the sea according to their needs.

From the beginning of the Formative Epoch the elements of the cultural pattern spread rapidly throughout the territory of Peru, contributing to the formation of the local cultures. Everywhere the seeds germinated vigorously and led to a flowering of different civilisations. The styles of painting and sculpture and architecture, the types of religious building, and the primitive conception of the image of divinity were taken over by the small local cultures and modified to satisfy their own particular artistic sense or to meet their particular material and spiritual needs. Thus were created the various cultures which developed so actively in the Formative Epoch, during which human energy and inventiveness contributed such a powerful impetus to the generation of fresh conceptions in a new world.

Vicus   *(Plates 12, 117, 130, 132)*

The latest discoveries at Vicus and the excavations at Virú have opened up new horizons in the study of this period, which is of such prime importance in the development of the cultures of Peru. Vicus can be seen as a cultural arrow directed from the Santa Catalina valley, Chicama and Virú towards the dunes of Vicus with their carob-trees and the other sites between Vicus and Ayabaca. We find the same sequence at Vicus during the Formative Epoch as in the Virú valley, and the civilisation attains its peak during stages I and II of the great Mochica culture.

Vicus is the most important centre of hand-made pottery in Peru. This type of pottery, found only in the Virú valley in forms similar to those of Vicus in the early period of the Formative Epoch, is classed by me as Pre-Cupisnique. Unfortunately neither the clandestine diggers nor the excavators from the National Museum were able to find bones or organic material which would have made it possible to date the various stages of Vicus. There is no doubt that we can identify at Vicus a whole range of types, from completely undecorated pots to "white-on-red" pottery like that found at Salinar in the Chicama valley, Santa Catalina and Virú. There is pottery without decoration, pottery with light incised lines, pottery with negative and positive decoration, pottery with motifs in white-on-red but with negative painting converted into positive, and finally the typical white-on-red pottery.

But although we have pottery at Vicus we do not, unfortunately, know what objects it was associated with – metals, stones, semi-precious stones, and so on. The excavators say that since the tombs were at a considerable depth the bodies had disintegrated and largely been absorbed into the soil. As we have already noted, no one has been able to correlate the many objects found from time to time with the pottery types of the various cultures found at Vicus; and Vicus is important because the pottery found there includes the principal types found in north Peru (i.e. mainly vessels with stirrup spouts) and in the south (vessels with a spout and a handle, or two spouts joined by a bridge). Moreover pots with flat handles have also been found – a type which only appears thousands of years later in the Huari culture. The most remarkable feature, however, was the finding at Vicus of the original forms of the stirrup-spouted and spout-and-bridge jars, throwing light on a problem which had puzzled the experts since the beginnings of Peruvian archaeology. This fact, and the fact that moulds had not yet been invented and the pottery was made by hand, convince me that we are here dealing with a very early period.

Some scholars have suggested that the stirrup spout which is characteristic of the pottery of northern Peru came from outside the country, since we have not been able to follow the development of the type. At Vicus, however, we find it not only on jars representing human heads but also on jars made in the form of the whole human body. The heads, forming bottle-shaped vessels, have a slightly sloping spout, and the handle runs from the spout to the forehead. Later the spout becomes curved, forming one end of the stirrup handle, and one of the ends is supported on the forehead by a solid handle for greater strength. In the final stage the solid handle is replaced by a hollow pipe, and we then have the stirrup spout. A very similar development is found in the jars representing the whole o a human body.

The first form of the spout-and-bridge jar is a round vessel representing a head, with a spout at the rear joined to a round handle. In the second stage one side of the handle is joined to the animal's head, which forms the front of the jar; and in the third the other end of the handle is raised and joined to the spout to form the bridge.

These two discoveries are of fundamental importance in Peruvian archaeology, for they demonstrate the progressive development of pottery types in Peru, the stirrup spout leading to the pottery characteristic of the northern cultures like Cupisnique, Salinar and Mochica, the spout-and-bridge jar to the pottery of the southern cultures like Paracas, Nazca and Huari. There is thus no ground for considering these types as coming from outside Peru.

In the Virú valley I found the same progressive development of pottery. The sherds of hand-made pottery are very similar to those I classify as Pre-Cupisnique. I recall a stirrup-spouted jar found in the Marañón area, a piece of hand-made pottery of very similar type. It is coarse ware with poorly modelled features and not a trace of colour, recalling the hand-worked pottery of Vicus and Virú.

In my book *La Ceramica de Vicus* I put this period between Pre-Cupisnique and Cupisnique, dating it earlier than Cupisnique.

So far we are unable to say anything about the civilisations of this stage. We do not possess the contents of the tombs, and know nothing of the architecture. We cannot say which particular kinds of pottery were found in the different types of tomb for, as I have already observed, there are no scientific data which could provide reference points. We do, however, find agriculture beginning to develop at this stage.

The feline which we have already found in its animal form now becomes stylised, though it still retains the characteristic feline body; the mouth becomes larger and the lips are disproportionately thickened; the teeth protrude from the mouth in the form of fangs, or are elaborately interlaced. In other examples the feline has a large tongue which protrudes from its mouth and curls upwards to its nose; the eyes are usually represented by a circle in relief with a slit in the centre. It is interesting to note that when these felines are drawn in profile they have a very marked resemblance to the incised representations of the feline at Cupisnique and in other cultures of the same period. The round eye with a cavity in the centre readily develops into the typical eye found in the stylised felines of the Chavín culture; and the grotesquely exaggerated tongue is to be compared with the tongue which serves as a connection between two stylised feline heads in the decoration of some specimens of incised ware. This suggests that these figures are indications of a cult of the stylised feline which became general in later cultures and crystallised in the Chavín temple and the splendid stelae associated with it.

Thus it was in this phase of the Formative Epoch, when the various cultures were beginning to take shape, that the indigenous civilisations took their first steps. Although at present we know only primitive centres for the production of hand-made pottery I am sure that some day, when proper excavations have been carried out, we shall find in Peru a stratum of pottery with incised patterns and decorated with terracotta knobs and ridges, as well as hand-made pottery in a variety of forms according to the place of manufacture. It took a great many years to reach the stage—one of immense significance—when these cultures took their first steps; and there is still a hiatus to be filled between the peoples who had pottery of the Queneto type and peoples like those of the Pre-Cupisnique stage and the beginnings of the Vicus culture.

Later these cultures developed out of the primitive stage and took on their own individualities. Then the crude strivings of the earlier phase are replaced by a determined effort to progress, demonstrated by the inventive spirit which these cultures display and by their constant attempt to better their previous achievements.

Cupisnique

This phenomenon is seen in a number of developments which rapidly spread throughout the country, contributing to the cultural progress of each group. Incised and relief decoration are found at Nepeña, and these styles also extend to

Sechín, Paracas, Cupisnique, Morropón, Chongoyape, Huánuco and Chanapata. In all these areas the incised decoration is used to embellish not only pottery but also bone objects and articles in everyday use.

Thus we find art reaching out to cover the whole of Peru. The type of the feline develops and becomes more stylised, and we find the first signs of the humanisation of the feline god. Throughout Peru we find these representations of the feline, along with figures of minor deities—the condor, the owl and the snake.

The metals had not yet been discovered, and bone was used to make a variety of implements such as spoons, spatulas and awls, as well as rings, ear-rings, and so on. When something stronger was needed stone was used—to make, for example, mortars or vessels of various kinds. Stone was also used for carving figures of deities, jet for making mirrors, beads for necklaces and various containers. The men of this period wore caps and loincloths, and adorned themselves with fine necklaces, bracelets and breastplates made of turquoise, lapis lazuli, bone, shells or other materials. Their religious feelings were centred even more strongly on the feline, so that some scholars have been led into the error of seeing this stage as a theocratic empire: in fact it was merely the spiritual upsurge of peoples who had embraced with fervour the cult of the semi-humanised feline. *(Plates 97, 145)*

The cult of the dead, too, shows new practices. The bodies were buried in a flexed position and covered with a red pigment—though this does not mean, as some have suggested, that they were secondary burials. Round the skeletons are found jars with religious motifs, jars in the shape of human beings, animals or plants, mortars, mirrors and other objects. The dead were placed in the centre of the tomb, covered with an undecorated cloth and wearing their finest jewels.

Agriculture had now made some progress. We find representations of various fruits, and of tubers which were carefully cultivated such as manioc, potatoes and sweet potatoes.

In the coastal area the houses often had a stone base, and were built of conical adobe bricks of varying size—though the use of these bricks created serious technical problems. The same materials were used for building tombs. To strengthen the walls of their buildings they used large field stones laid without mortar, filling in the gaps with smaller stones. The Cupisniques also built circular fortresses and temples in the form of a pyramid. At Punkurí, for example, the walls are painted in delicate colours, with red, blue and green predominating. A large feline which crowns the temple is also painted in many colours. The pottery, baked in closed kilns, is poorly fired and the material is not properly selected, but it is well polished and finely shaped. In the pottery of this period we note a vigorous advance; but it is mainly the art of sculpture which now emerges in full splendour, making headway particularly in northern Peru where it followed the incised decoration, at the same time as the cultures of Paracas, Cupisnique, Morropón and other areas were developing. Now for the first time in Peru we find colour applied to pottery, always within areas clearly marked out by incised lines. In the north the prevalent colours are black and brown; in the south the range of colouring is much richer. The main sites where brown incised pottery and its derivatives have been found are Morropón, Vicus, the Air Base, the Chicama valley, Virú, Santa Catalina, Chao, Santa, San Jacinto, Nepeña, Ancón, Lima, Paracas, Chanapata, and Huancayo. *(Plates 4, 6, 9, 10)*

We were able to put together a fairly complete picture of the civilisations characterised by incised decoration. In the excavations at Barbacoa in the Chicama valley and at Santa Catalina and Virú where we discovered the Cupisnique civilisation we were able to find in the tombs all the material necessary to answer our questions, and could thus describe and define the characteristics of these various peoples. The results of this work were published in my book *Los Cupisniques*. Some test digging was done at Santa, Chongopaye, Nepeña and elsewhere, but Barbacoa was the only site to yield the necessary data. The Japanese scientific expedition which worked at Cotosh also produced an abundant supply of material.

Nepeña
The Nepeña valley deserves a chapter to itself in the story of the development of this period. It is undoubtedly one of the most important centres of the Formative Epoch, mainly because of its marvellous temples built of conical adobes, with walls covered with fine polychrome painting.

Dr. Tello excavated the Punkurí temple, finding a burial containing a mortar with its stone pestle. On the summit of the temple was a remarkable figure of a seated feline, which showed a considerable degree of stylisation though still preserving the characteristics of the animal. Another magnificent building in this valley is the Cerro Blanco temple, belonging to a stage later than the banded relief, i.e. the Chavín period.

32, 33 →

34   35

37

38, 39 →

40

41

The men of this period possessed the architectural skill and the artistic bent to achieve such splendid buildings as these, with their imposing layout and the painted decoration in many colours on religious themes which covered the walls of the temples. The Nepeña culture is not confined to the valley of that name but extends into the Sechín valley. The temple in this valley is remarkable in other respects: its walls are built up from large and small stones alternately, and are decorated with bas-reliefs belonging to a very primitive phase of the Formative Epoch. Most of these represent warriors: stylised heads, such as were also used to represent religious personages at this period. The Mojeque temple in the Casma valley has on its walls monumental sculptured figures representing mythical beings, works of genuine artistic achievement by men who were masters not only of sculpture but of polychrome painting. In my view these structures, like those of Cerro Blanco, belong not to the Formative but to the Florescent Epoch, for they show the development of art already reaching maturity.

The only valleys where we find such striking differences are the Casma and Nepeña valleys. So far it has unfortunately been impossible to discover any cemeteries, although innumerable sherds from pottery of this period have been found. Other objects discovered in this area were the gold dishes, the globular gold vessel with a double spout and bridge, and another dish, which are now to be seen in the Rafael Larco Herrera Museum. It is clear from all this that this culture had passed out of the Formative Epoch into the Florescent Epoch; and this is confirmed by its architecture. We know nothing of its pottery, apart from a single terracotta object from Casma in the Rafael Larco Herrera Museum and another found by a private person at Nepeña.

It is surprising that we find architectural remains but no tombs. The tombs are of course very difficult to discover: it took me twelve years to find Cupisnique, though I had sometimes as many as a hundred men helping me in my search.

The importance of the architecture found in this area and the development that can be seen in the arts of painting and sculpture suggest to me that this was the centre from which came the style and the religious beliefs which spread through the whole of Peru. It is significant that if we go farther up the Nepeña valley we come to Chavín, the masterpiece of the style of the Formative Epoch in its full flowering. I am convinced, therefore, as I have already said, that this was the religious centre which gave rise to the cult of the feline at the period when the style of incised decoration came to the fore during the Florescent Epoch.

Ancón and Paracas Cavernas

Most of the vases found in the Ancón area are of a quite different type from those found at Cupisnique. Many have had a black slip applied to them, and thus belong to a later stage than Cupisnique. They usually have large geometric patterns, which are differentiated from the rest of the jar by stippling, hatching, cross-hatching or roughening. The commonest shapes are flat, cylindrical, globular, or in the form of a truncated cone. Some of the jars are red; some are double, with a circular spout and bridge; one – a departure from the usual geometrical shape – is a small black figurine.

The men of this period lived in caves near the sea and were fishermen. They laid out their dead on a mat, setting offerings made of wickerwork near the head or round the body. Among the objects found here are very beautiful carved wooden boxes, cylindrical vessels of stone, bone spatulas, and the jars already mentioned. There are also wooden dishes, rectangular containers, and boxes with religious motifs very different from those found at Cupisnique and other sites of this period. It was only at Ancón and Paracas that the inhabitants went in for basket-work, making not only baskets for everyday use but also objects in the shape of a hat. They also worked bone and stone, using the former to make needles, scrapers, beads and occasionally ornaments. As in all the cultures of this period, we also find stone objects resembling dishes, sometimes with three feet, as well as pestles and mortars and stone loom-weights.

Farther south, in the Paracas peninsula, Dr. Tello found remains of the Paracas civilisation, which in his view belongs to what he calls the Chavín civilisation or derives from it. Here there was pottery earlier than Paracas Cavernas, brown in colour, with incised decoration, but imperfectly fired. In this we can see something of the shapes of Paracas Cavernas pottery but without its refinement.

Paracas Cavernas does indeed correspond to the cultures of the Formative Epoch. It is given this name because the pottery was found associated with burials in caves, which were entered through a tunnel, usually built of stone. Inside the caves were the remains of the dead and the funerary offerings. These tombs are found in considerable numbers; sometimes they were clearly family tombs used for successive burials.

The subdivision of the different stages of the Paracas culture has been carried too far: in reality not more than four can properly be distinguished, the other divisions being related to different sites rather than to differences in the style itself.

I do not agree with those who maintain that a jar has only to have a stirrup spout or a representation of the feline to be counted among the most ancient. The jars with handles, spouts and bridges do not belong either to the Chavín or the Cupisnique phase: clearly they are to be assigned to a late period. This is shown by the handles, which resemble those of the Mochica I period; they are not so thick as those characteristic of the middle phase of the Formative Epoch, which have a large rim like that found in pottery of the same type from Huancayo, Morropón, the transitional period at Santa, and the Chavín temple itself.

The stylisation of the feline has made no further progress, and it is thus closer to the religious conception which we observe in the Mochica I period. In one of the representations from an early period in the Rafael Larco Herrera Museum, and in other representations I have seen in private collections, the feline – still in animal form – has the three points on its head which are typical of the Chongoyape feline. Some jars show us a feline which is already anthropomorphic. In my view this form is later than the representation of the feline as an animal, although the latter is more stylised. The fact that the pottery has patterns of Chavín type does not necessarily make it older than other types; for we find that during the Mochica III period pottery is decorated with motifs from the Chavín temple. For this reason I still stand by the classification which I worked out twenty years ago; and in this I put the pottery of Pinilla last, although it may be earlier than the pottery of Paracas Necrópolis.

In certain other areas like the Nazca valley, particularly at Ica, on the Hacienda Ocucaje and in the Palpa valley, burials have been found in irregularly shaped pits of the normal type; some have also been found in caves, the walls of which were lined with a mixture of straw and earth.

The pottery has all the characteristics of the Formative Epoch. It is poorly fired, and is covered with incised decoration, mainly of religious significance. Instead of applying a thin layer of paint in liquid or powder form before firing, the potters applied a thick layer of paint after firing, which gave it the appearance of oil painting. Curiously enough, some of the Paracas Cavernas shapes are also found at Vicus, Salinar and Virú; for example the globular jars with a double spout and bridge, or the head-shaped jars with a spout and bridge. The latter type has a very characteristic feature which suggests a relationship between the two cultures – a swelling at the base of the spout which is found only at Vicus and Paracas. Moreover, a number of jars have been found with decoration in the typical polychrome painting, and also some with negative decoration. Associated with this pottery have been found jars in shapes which are now considered typical of Paracas, with painted decoration. All those experts with long experience of the south of Peru whom I have consulted, such as Dr. Muelle, Sr Mejía Xespe and Sr Roselló, agree that the jars with negative decoration are not found alone but are associated with Paracas Cavernas pottery. This observation, combined with the fact that at Paracas we find the stirrup spout and at Vicus we find the principal types of Paracas pottery, leads to the conclusion that in Peru the cultural waves travelled from north to south. The typical colours of this pottery are a greenish-brown, red, black, pastel blue, white and yellow. *(Plate 109)*

There are some jars in which the pottery base is decorated with incised motifs, splendidly patterned and using a variety of techniques. In some cases the feline is very similar to the Cupisnique type; in others it diverges considerably from the northern conception and is much more like the type found at Chongoyape.

Small ornaments for clothing or turbans have also been found; they are made from thin gold plates, simple in form and without decoration.

This Paracas Cavernas culture, for which we have such limited evidence, is of importance in the south of Peru, for this was the people which later gave birth to the Nazca culture.

Incised Paracas
The pottery which I call "Incised Paracas" is similar in form to Cavernas, but is blackish-brown in colour because it was fired in closed kilns. It is decorated with large incised patterns, made up of combed, stippled or hatched motifs, to set off the different surfaces. Its technique and decoration are similar to those of Ancón pottery. At a later stage of its development this pottery was covered with a slip which gave it the appearance of a glaze, and the incised lines, instead of being cut when the clay was fairly hard, were drawn when it was still soft, giving the decoration something of the effect of a bas-relief.

Some gold objects were discovered in the Fárrate and the Chongoyape tombs. We must, therefore, classify these finds in the initial phase of the Florescent Epoch, because the style continued in these areas until then; though some pottery has also been found there which certain writers, rather lacking in proper scientific caution, call classic Chavín pottery and date to the Formative Epoch.

Chongoyape

The incised pottery of Chongoyape is different from that of Cupisnique or Ancón. If it is compared with Cupisnique the spouts and handles seem much thinner and of rather rectangular shape. The motifs of the reliefs show a difference in technique, as do the anthropomorphic vases and the models of circular houses which have been found here. There is a difference also in the animals, and in the decorative motifs. Similarly the decorations representing humans, animals or plants, which are much more numerous than at Cupisnique, show the progress that has already been achieved.

Transitional Cupisnique

After the blackish-brown pottery with incised decoration comes the coloured pottery. In the Chicama valley we find the pottery known as Cupisnique of Santa Ana which differs completely from the other types. The stirrup spout and handle are different; there is incised geometric decoration; and the feline, which was the main decorative theme of the pottery previously discussed, disappears as an ornamental motif. The art of pottery reached new heights, producing well-fired jars, usually red in colour. This pottery is found in graves of irregular shape, with furnishings which are similar to those of the preceding phase though inferior in quality. There are thus a number of stages corresponding to the different phases of pottery with incised decoration. *(Plates 5, 7)*

Later we find a stratum of pottery with negative decoration, which spreads throughout Peru like the earlier stratum, and we see the development of a new art of painting, giving full plastic expression to its subjects. Throughout this development we see new forms of pottery appearing and individual interpretations emerging; new techniques are discovered, and the cultural resources of the period are enriched.

Pottery with the type of decoration just described was found at Paracas in the tomb which contained the splendid cloaks which are associated throughout the archaeological world with the name of Paracas, and is also frequently found with the vases known as Paracas Necrópolis.

The negative decorated pottery of Vicus is particularly attractive. It continued to be worked by hand hundreds of years after moulds like those used at Virú had come into use. These terracotta jars from Vicus are of striking beauty, with a

65

cichness of form which reveals the work of genuine and dedicated artists. When rompared with the incised pottery they seem more like caricatures than real likenesses, but in their simplicity of style we see intimations of a real feeling for sculptural modelling.

It is in the pottery of Vicus that we find the first representation in Peru of a woman giving birth to a child, and we also have what seems to be the oldest representation of a man with his legs cut off, in a double jar showing a man with both legs amputated just above the knee.

We had already found the first musical instruments, like the drum, which seem to have been made in pottery. The favourite animals at this period were the llama, the roe-deer, the monkey, a kind of otter or weasel, the fox, and birds like owls, ducks, parrots and doves.

At Paracas negative painting was applied both externally and internally, particularly on flat dishes; it is also found on jars with double spout and bridge. But it has not been possible anywhere else to carry out excavations producing more concrete evidence about the contents of tombs with negative-decorated pottery. Virú, which belongs to the same phase, has magnificent temples and other buildings, but it is difficult to differentiate work of this period from buildings of the Florescent Epoch. In consequence we cannot say to what period the various temples and other buildings in this area belong.

In many cultures of this period the dead were buried in simple graves; in others sarcophagi of reeds or adobe were used. The cult of the dead became increasingly important, and in cult images we find the feline god represented as a feline, though with certain stylised features. Other representations of the feline show a stylised mouth with long fangs and prominent lips.

The peoples and cultures which used negative decoration were clearly of warlike disposition. Most of the weapons found at Vicus, for example, seem to have belonged to these peoples. The pottery itself shows warriors armed with shields and clubs designed to give both battering and penetrating wounds. From other evidence we know that they wore large breastplates and carried star-headed copper maces and small axes. They wore little in the way of clothing: most of them went naked or wore only a loincloth. Their headgear consisted of different types of cap, sometimes of a crown. It is interesting to observe that in the pottery of Vicus we find figures of women with their hair arranged in the same way as their descendants of today at Eten or Monsefu, their long tresses, whether plaited or hanging loose, being wound into a kind of turban tied by a cotton thread.

At both Virú and Chicama we are surprised to see what progress has been made in metal-working. The men of this period were not only able to work gold, from which they fashioned small tubes, hollow spheres, wire and plaques which served to make necklaces, nose ornaments or ear-rings: they also knew the technique of soldering and were beginning to do repoussé work. They also used copper, casting lance-points, maces, discs for crowns, small spangles and a variety of other ornaments. In the Virú valley the copper was gilded with a thick coating of gold. The objects found at Vicus came from tombs containing pottery with incised decoration; and here we find a new technique in which the object was coated with silver before being covered with gold. Evidently the people of Vicus were more skilled goldsmiths than the people of Virú.

We now come to the final period of the Formative Epoch, a stage which is full of interest. In this period we find a remarkable development of negative-painted pottery, not only in the decorative motifs but also in the shapes, which are of remarkable beauty. The pottery is no longer exclusively hand-made: moulds are now employed and we find their use extending throughout Peru, giving rise to another pan-Peruvian decorative style like the incised pottery already described. Although a certain amount of work has been done at Virú and Santa Catalina there has been no scientific investigation at Vicus; and we cannot, therefore, say anything about these cultures. All that we have to go on is the hand-made pottery with negative-painted decoration and the weapons, which – like the pottery and much of the other material found at Vicus – resemble those found at Virú.

Virú

We must now give a brief account of the culture of Virú. It is the only one on which we have any archaeological data, and consequently the only one where we can give any satisfactory answer to the problems posed by the surviving remains. It was in 1933 that I discovered this culture, the great importance of which has recently been realised; for it was the Virú culture that gave rise in the Florescent Epoch to the important culture of Santa (Callejón de Huaylas). The Virú culture also contributed something to the formation of the Mochica culture. Its pottery is found in the Chicama valley, at Santa Catalina, Chao and Santa as well as at Virú itself.

Virú is the second important centre for the production of negative-painted pottery. There is less hand-made pottery than at Vicus; most of it is modelled, and thus of greater artistic value. It is better finished and uses shapes not found at Vicus. Altogether the art of pottery had achieved greater refinement at Virú.

The people of Virú were of medium height, and seem to have been less vigorous than the Mochicas or Cupisniques. The skulls found are brachycephalic, dolichocephalic and mesocephalic, and are notable for the frequent occurence of wormian bones. I believe that these differences are due to the fact that the tombs found belong to the Formative Epoch and the beginning of the Florescent Epoch. In some tombs skulls were found showing attempts to achieve cranial deformation of the direct tabular type.

In the pottery we find representations of manioc, sweet potatoes, zapote (a fruit resembling a cucumber, *Calocarpum mammosum*), lucumas and gourds. In the tombs were remains of groundnuts, beans, maize, red beans, squashes and a black seed which has not been identified. As domestic animals we find roe-deer, monkeys and parrots. There are no scenes of hunting or fishing, though there are representations of some of the mammals, birds, fish or shellfish which must have been used for food. There are also representations of the reed raft, which show that it was already in use; and as funerary offerings we find conches, snails and nautilus shells, indicating that these were also used for food.

Like the inhabitants of Vicus, the men of Virú wore only a small loincloth and adorned themselves with crowns and large circular ear ornaments. They too plaited their hair with cords, arranging it so that one plait hung down on each side of their head. Their crowns and ear ornaments might have as many as three pendants, usually wire rings with a large ear-drop. They wore necklaces of stone, turquoise or lapis lazuli – a modest type of ornament compared with that of the Mochicas or Cupisniques. They also had gold necklaces made up of small hollow balls, and cylindrical ear ornaments in openwork. They were fascinated by music and played the drum, the Pan pipes and the flute. They tattooed their faces, and I have found cases where the tattoo paint had penetrated into the skull at the edge of the eye socket. We do not know whether they drank *chicha*, but there are representations of people chewing coca leaves.

They may have used *achango* as a medicine. One skull I found was most skilfully trepanned: its owner had suffered from a disease which the doctor had treated by boring a number of small holes about the diameter of a pencil. The skull also showed what I believe to be the earliest bone graft known in ancient times.

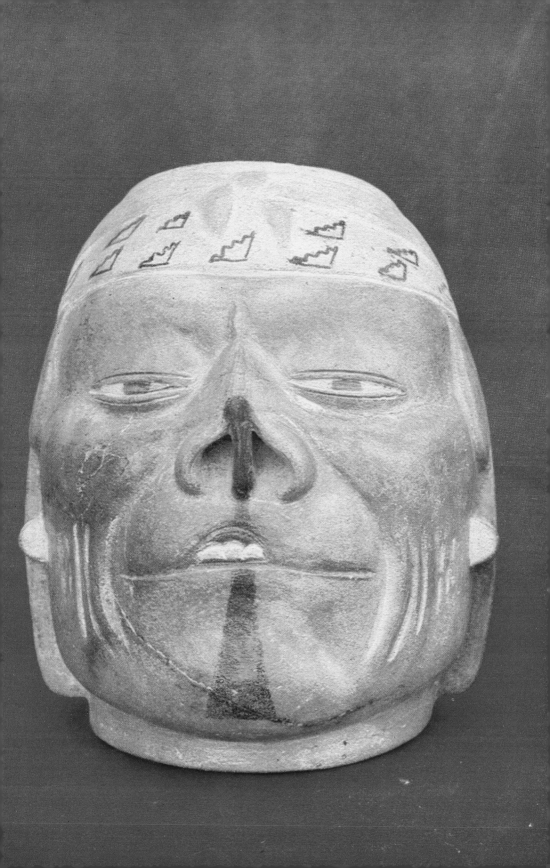

46, 47, 48 →

45

←42, 43, 44,

50, 51, 52→

49

What little cloth they used was woven with a slack warp. The needles that have been found bear witness to the meagreness of their clothing.

It was a warlike race. The warriors carried small square or rectangular shields and were armed with maces of stone or copper, which were sometimes gilded or ornamented with lapis lazuli. As a rule they were blunt instruments with a copper spike at the end. *(Plates 23, 103)*

The people of Virú were magnificent architects, and most of the buildings in the Virú valley belong to this culture. The representations of houses in the pottery show the progress achieved in this field, and indeed the style of building is not very different from the ideas of our own day. The houses have pitched roofs, disposed in such a way as to allow light and air to reach the interior at different times of day. The arrangement of the wide window bays, particularly on the upper floor, is a remarkable achievement for the period. The windows were either square, rectangular or trapezoidal in shape. The roof ridge might be either plain or decorated; where there was a flat roof it was often supported by pillars. The door was arched.

The Virú culture thus surpassed the culture of Vicus in every respect. The pottery in particular is superior, showing a great variety of refined forms which are peculiar to Virú. The spouts are very small and the handles carefully rounded.

The Virú pottery is similar to that of the other cultures. There are representations of men, animals and plants, of houses and of felines; and the potters seem to have felt a particular urge to model feet and hands. There are containers in the shape of bottles and conches. The principal types include stirrup-spouted jars, jars with double spout and bridge, double jars with a handle and a bridge, bottles with a handle, globular vessels with a neck, and flared jars. *(Plates 11, 24, 27)*

As at Vicus, the modelling is primitive, only the main part of the jar being made in a mould. As a rule the potter was not interested in the human figure, delineating the hands and feet in a very summary way. The representations of animals, on the other hand, are particularly fine.

The decoration of the pottery is by negative painting. The patterns are carefully drawn, particularly in the finer pottery which represents the highest stage of this culture. The motifs are mostly geometric – parallel lines, serrated lines, circles, volutes and triangles. The starfish, with its curving tentacles, is a common theme. As a rule the whole surface of the jar was decorated.

The people of Virú were skilled metal-workers, able to produce metal sheet, to solder, to do repoussé and openwork. Their gilding was of the highest quality. Metal objects were found in the tombs containing moulded pottery but not in those with hand-made pottery.

There are few representations of the feline, but when it does appear it is shown in animal form, slightly stylised. The lips are drawn apart to show the teeth protruding from the mouth, giving the creature an expression of greater ferocity.

There is a remarkable and interesting development of the cult of the dead. Tombs of different types have been found, including stone sarcophagi and graves in which the dead were stretched out on their backs.

The Virú culture, as we have already noted, achieved increasing importance: in the Virú valley the Florescent Epoch continued into the Mochica I and II periods. It flourished particularly in the Santa valley, giving rise to the Santa culture, one of the most interesting of the Florescent Epoch. *(Plate 13)*

In the south of Peru negative-painted pottery is represented by the jars known as Paracas Necrópolis, and also by the jars with incised and negative-painted decoration in many colours belonging to the Paracas Cavernas culture. Elsewhere 'n Peru we have only the jars found in a small number of tombs in a number of different areas, a few ruins and cemetery areas, and a considerable quantity of sherds. In the Santa valley, for example, the negative-painted pottery is closely related to that found in the Virú valley.

These discoveries make it possible to say that this decorative style is pan-Peruvian. But scientific excavations have been conducted – both by the author of the present work and by American archaeologists – in only one area, the Virú, Santa Catalina and Chicama valleys. It is thus possible to discuss the Virú culture on the basis of proper scientific data. The finds made at Virú do no more, however, than prepare the way for a comparative typological study of the pottery. It is unfortunate that, in spite of the quantity of material available, we do not possess sufficient concrete data to establish on the ground the chronological succession of the pottery types and the association with the pottery of the many metal and other objects found in this area.

Nevertheless these two great centres of negative-painted pottery reveal the influence of negative painting on Peruvian decorative art; for the various cultures which flourished throughout Peru adopted this type of decoration and made it their own. And it is interesting to see how at each successive stage of the development of pottery we find it producing similar forms. We must note, however, that although there are similar forms at Vicus and Virú and even at Paracas, where we find jars with the double spout and bridge and head-shaped jars with spout and bridge, we also see differentiating features in the pottery found at different places. At the same time we find, during the period of incised decoration, common features like negative-painted decoration, the representation of the feline in certain types of pottery and metal objects, and so on.

Negative decoration was a discovery of prime importance in the artistic development of ancient Peru. It remained in use for several centuries and was then followed by the first experiments in the use of positive painting.

The cultures with pottery decorated in white-on-red are found mainly in the Chicama valley, at Salinar, at Virú, Santa, Lima, Nazca and elsewhere. The best site for studying the pottery is Vicus; for a general study of the cultures concerned the best sites are the Chicama valley, Virú and Santa.

At first positive decoration was applied on top of negative decoration at Vicus, with no attempt to combine the two. In some cases one type of painting is found above the other, and sometimes the positive painting covers some lines left by the under-painting in order to achieve a more striking effect. Later, in the same type of pottery, negative motifs are converted into positive, though the decoration is fairly coarse. On pottery with a red base the pattern is picked out in white. The decorative motifs – lines, circles and so on – are similar to those used in negative decoration. Later the pottery achieves increased refinement, and we then find the local type of white-on-red decoration appearing at Vicus. Jars with white painting combined with negative decoration are very rare at Virú, in the Chicama valley and at Santa. With the passage of time the negative painting is transformed into positive painting, in the style known as Virú of Chicama. Here, however, the motifs are painted in black rather than white, though they are found at the same time as the positive painting in white. The pottery which I call Salinar, with motifs in white-on-red, extends throughout Peru, constituting a new artistic style which begins at the same time as the negative painting technique but then develops in its purest form quite separately from negative decoration. Positive painting thus becomes predominant, and then becomes the sole decorative style employed in Peruvian pottery.

Salinar

The Salinar culture, which I discovered in the Chicama valley in 1941, has distinctive characteristics of its own. The red pottery, in the natural colour of the baked clay, with forms different from those with which we have hitherto been concerned, shows a unity of style indicating that it belonged to a distinctive culture. This material was discovered at Salinar, in the upper Chicama valley, near the cemeteries of the Cupisnique culture. I found a series of levels, one after the other – Salinar tombs on top of Cupisnique tombs, and Mochica tombs above Salinar tombs – which make it possible to establish the chronological sequence of these cultures.

We note at once that the art of pottery has made progress. The materials have been chosen with care, and the quality of the paste and the firing has been much improved. The colour is now fairly uniform: evidently the pottery was baked in open fires rather than closed kilns. Some vases are polished, though most of them have the natural dull finish of the terracotta. Moulds are used, and white and red painting is applied to bring out the pattern. The bottle-shaped jar is predominant, but stirrup-spouted vessels are also found; and, as usual, there are representations of humans, animals and other subjects. At Salinar we also find geometric motifs, and in some jars the painting is laid on between incised lines. *(Plates 26, 28, 29)*

Five spatulas with religious motifs, belonging to the Cupisnique culture, were found at the same place. It must be said, however, that these themes have lost any real meaning: they are merely an attempt to reproduce the motifs found on earlier Cupisnique spatulas.

The pottery was decorated with the brush, using white paint: here we find the beginnings of the art of positive painting. In sculpture, however, there seems to have been a regression, though we can perceive an attempt to give the objects and animals represented a more natural appearance and more harmonious proportions. The artists are concerned to record the natural appearance and attitudes of the animals they depict – though they seem to have a tendency to reproduce whatever part interests them most, not always achieving complete precision.

At this stage the use of stone for sculpture disappears.

We found two fine representations of houses. One is a modest dwelling with a pitched roof, with window bays decorated with step-shaped pillars. The other is a tower, with similar window bays and a very handsome frieze of interlaced ribbons. The houses, tombs and fortresses of the people of Salinar were built of adobe bricks in the shape of spherical domes – a style adopted because of the difficulty of building with conical bricks.

The people of Salinar wore hats made of straw, and the women arranged their hair in a coiffure made up of successive layers of tresses. Sometimes they were tattooed. Curiously enough we find no representations of clothes in the pottery, apart from some jars which suggest that they wore a kind of long shift. They also wore very simple ear ornaments and necklaces made of turquoise, stones, shells and terracotta. None of these objects, however, are of the same standard as those found at Cupisnique. Fragments of cloth of the usual type, made with separate webs, are also found, along with wooden or bone needles.

The Salinar people wore discs of sheet gold and were beginning to understand the making of alloys. Seeds of gourds, maté and maize are found among the funerary offerings, and the cactus begins to appear on the pottery. Organic matter and meat has been found in the gourds; we find also clams, *pámpanos* and mussels; and the llama was also known.

In this stage the cult of the feline seems to disappear, and we find only sculptured representations of the animal. This suggests that the Cupisniques of Santa Ana may have adopted this form of worship.

In our investigations here we found the earliest known representation of a doctor tending the sick, as well as the earliest erotic scenes known in Peru, or for that matter in the world: or so at any rate we must suppose so long as it has not been possible to date the pottery of Vicus.[1]

The cult of the dead now develops in a form different from that previously practised. The mode of burial becomes uniform: the body is usually stretched out with the legs extended and sometimes crossed, half turned on to its right side, being

[1] Those interested in this subject may care to read my *Checan* (Nagel, 1965)

maintained in this position with the help of stones. The tombs were pits in the shape of an elongated ellipse; and the bodies were placed along the wall of the tomb and covered with stone slabs in a kind of sarcophagus. There were also multiple burials.

The white-on-red pottery of the Santa valley is different from the pottery of the same type found at Salinar. The few jars of this culture which have been found have lipped spouts like the jars of the Mochica period instead of the straight-rimmed spouts found at Salinar. There is also a striking difference in the motifs used. Among the Virú jars we found some in a dark colour, almost blackish-brown, showing strong Cupisnique influence. A more refined type of pottery is found at Chiclayo and at Vicus, the second important centre of white-on-red pottery. These jars are completely different from the Salinar type and represent a more refined development of the negative-painted jars. They are produced with the help of moulds, and are decorated with a very advanced positive painting technique.

The modelling also develops and the texture of the jars improves. It is clear that the materials have been properly selected, and the firing is much superior to that of the negative-painted pottery. The representations of human beings, animals and plants are much more skilfully done, with a greater degree of realism – though the extremities of arms and legs are crudely indicated in schematic cylindrical form.

As we have shown, the forms found in negative-decorated pottery continue to be used. Thus we find jars with a spout and a handle, jars with double spout and bridge, bottle-shaped handled vessels, and head-shaped spout-and-bridge jars.

The men of this culture still went naked, but they wore handsome head-dresses and ear ornaments, and arranged their hair in complicated tresses. They wore breastplates, sometimes quite small, sometimes large. The material found in the tombs does not allow us to say any more than this about their way of life.

White-on-red jars have been found in excavations at Lima, Chancay, Huaraz, Nazca, Palpa, Cuzco, Huari and Callejón de Huaylas. They form a stratum in which the art of positive painting is born and a high standard of beauty is achieved by the peoples of the Formative Epoch of Peruvian civilisation. And alongside this development in artistic methods we find a spread of new inventions in other fields, as man strives with all his might to emerge from the night of ignorance.

We find a growth in man's knowledge and in his command of the arts and sciences, both in the spiritual and in the material domain. In this way the cultures which sought with so much effort to reach out beyond their earlier achievements each made their contribution to the gradual crystallisation of the cultures which later reached their culmination in the Florescent Epoch. Their great merit is to have prepared the way for the great cultures which were to leave their indelible imprint on the classical epoch of Peruvian civilisation.

The Mochica Complex

After the white-on-red period in the north of Peru – at Vicus and in the Chicama valley, at Santa Catalina and Virú – the various elements which have been mentioned begin to come together to form what I call the Mochica complex: in effect, all these important cultures of the Formative Epoch begin to amalgamate. We find jars with incised decoration, others with negative painting, the first jars with sculptural modelling – in short, a variety of types from all the different cultures. Many of them are neither painted nor polished; then later we see refined and perfected types appearing during the early Mochica period. This period is the crucible in which all the different elements fuse and crystallise in the orange ware produced in the full flowering of the northern cultures. There is also an intermediate stage which I have been unable to define, for it is found only in an isolated form which is difficult to distinguish from Mochica pottery of the first period. In the cemetery of Virú de Santa Ana I had previously found a piece of orange ware associated with a negative-painted jar.

Orange Ware

This orange ware was discovered by the author of the present work in 1946 in tombs along with Virú pottery and orange-coloured jars with motifs painted in cream, particularly in the Santa Catalina and Virú valleys. At first I was inclined to assign them to the Mochica I period on account of their lipped spouts. Later, however, when all the specimens were brought together they were seen to be different from Mochica I jars, being coloured orange with cream decoration while the Mochica jars were cream with decoration in orange. Among these jars were many which had a considerable likeness to the negative-painted jars of Virú and Vicus, with a spout and bridge instead of a handle. They were like the negative-painted ware also by including representations of human beings and animals. At Vicus, alongside jars of identical or very similar shape to the pottery with negative decoration, we found orange-coloured jars with decoration in cream which are clearly the precursors of this type. And what seems to me even more important is that some of the jars which are identical in form to those with white-on-red positive decoration are often found as precursors of the orange-coloured jars with cream decoration. *(Plates 25, 112)*

This pottery is strikingly beautiful in form and can be compared with the finest productions of the Mochica period. We find in it a combination of the classical Mochica forms and those of the negative-painted pottery of Vicus of the last period. In general this pottery is figurative, representing animals, for example, in every detail; but we also find pieces which display a vein of fancy and considerable imaginative power.

In this phase, as in the Mochica I period, we sometimes find the same mould used to produce a whole series of pieces: a practice never adopted in the Chicama or Santa Catalina valleys or the other neighbouring valleys. In the Department of La Libertad it is very rare to find two copies of the same jar: it seems to have been the custom to break the mould after the jar was completed. At Vicus, on the other hand, we sometimes find as many as twenty jars from the same mould.

We cannot say anything about the metal-working or the architecture of this culture, or about the contents of the tombs with the orange ware, for we find the same situation here as with the other tombs at Vicus.

Cultures analogous to the Mochica complex must, I think, have existed in other parts of Peru before the flowering of the cultures in the Florescent Epoch. In the present state of knowledge this cannot be shown for the south of Peru or the Andes area; but I believe that the solution I have been able to put forward, after prolonged study and thought, accords with the archaeological evidence and provides an answer to questions which have remained unsettled for so many years.

Thus we reach the end of our study of a period which may not, perhaps, equal the Florescent Epoch in artistic achievement or in material progress but is nevertheless important as the time when, by persistent and devoted effort, the foundations were laid for the greater cultures that were to follow.

It is fair to say that if the production of pottery with incised decoration is the mark of an empire then we must give this title also to the peoples with negative-painted pottery and to those who produced pottery with white-on-red decoration.

If incised decoration is the hallmark of a culture, then so is negative decoration or white-on-red. And if incised decoration defines a pan-Peruvian horizon, so equally do negative decoration and white-on-red. I am not one of those who believe in one or other of the four theoretical possibilities without any sufficient basis for their belief. The explanation to which I firmly adhere is much simpler and more closely related to the facts. We are concerned here merely with decorative styles which extend throughout the whole of Peru along with all the various products of human inventiveness which develop and accumulate to give shape to the pan-Peruvian cultures of this epoch.

We must not forget that this is a formative epoch; and, remembering this, we can contemplate the unfolding panorama of the cultures which ebb and flow across the territory of Peru, constantly in quest of new directions and new discoveries which may point the way to higher cultural achievement.

THE FLORESCENT EPOCH

IV

The cultural elements created by the peoples of the Formative Epoch prepared the way for the crystallisation and blossoming of the great civilisations of the Florescent Epoch. The various cultures whose pottery was characterised in the Formative Epoch by the three pan-Peruvian artistic styles which have been described all contributed their share to this development; and one of them left an indelible imprint on the Florescent Epoch.

Lambayeque

Thus in the north of Peru we find the Vicus civilisation on the Hacienda Pabur site in the Department of Piura; and traces of it are thought also to have been found at Ayabaca. The Vicus culture is characterised by negative-painted pottery, the typical jars in the incised Vicus style, and the white-on-red jars found in the same locality. As we see in the Chicama valley, the Mochica civilisation was born of the fusion of these three elements. Nevertheless, as we have noted, there are differences in the pottery and in the other manifestations of these cultures. When we come to the Mochica II period we find that the Mochica culture does not follow the natural course of development observed in the Chicama valley, but disappears.

A culture cannot, however, disappear as suddenly as this. A little farther to the south is the Department of Lambayeque; and if we examine the Mochica II pottery found at Vicus we see that this pottery is cream-coloured with red lines, like the pottery which I call Lambayeque I and assign to the first period of the Florescent Epoch of this pottery. A study of the pottery forms of Vicus and Lambayeque leads me to conclude that the Lambayeque culture originated in the Mochica II period of Vicus; for in it we find not only the colouring but also the types – the vessels in the form of human faces with a spout and bridge, the vessels with double spout and bridge, the double jars with spout and bridge, the bottle-shaped vessels, and so on – which characterise the pottery of Vicus in the Formative Epoch. *(Plates 70, 71)*

I believe, therefore, that a colony was established at Vicus in the Formative Epoch and that the same elements contributed to its development as constituted the Mochica culture, with the addition of certain features peculiar to that culture.

There is no doubt that Vicus was dominated by the people of Virú, Santa Catalina and Chicama. Both in their pottery and in their goldsmith's work they had a number of elements in common, though there were also certain elements that differentiated them. In the Mochica II period the colony at Vicus did not follow the same line of development as the one in the Chicama valley, thus indicating that this particular people differed from the others and formed a political unit with distinctive features of its own in its religion, its arts and its architecture.

In studying the cultures of the Florescent Epoch we shall describe them in order, starting from the north and travelling southward along the coast; and we shall then follow the same system with the cultures of the highlands.

I do not propose to discuss the culture of Tumbes. Although the pottery of this area is not without interest it has not so far proved of sufficient importance to justify a special section. I shall begin, therefore, with the Lambayeque culture.

So far three phases have been identified: Lambayeque I, II and III. In the first the pottery is cream-coloured with red decoration; in the second it has the same colours, with polychrome motifs covering the whole surface of the jar; in the third – and in my opinion clearly the latest – the jars are red with cream decoration. As potters, the men of Lambayeque had not the mastery of modelling or the artistic genius of the Mochicas, but they did produce some interesting pieces. There are jars with representations of animals or plants, and others on religious themes; and there are also crude figures of human beings with rudimentary limbs, of no artistic value. Some of them clearly show Mochica influence and in these – though they are still far below the standard of the Mochica jars – we see a notable improvement in modelling skill.

The Indians of this period were skilled goldsmiths. The tombs of Batán Grande have acquired world renown because of the quantity and quality of the gold objects deposited in them as funerary offerings which have been found in the burial chambers. They are masterpieces of the goldsmith's craft. The craftsmen of Batán Grande could solder copper alloys and do engraving, repoussé and openwork; they combined gold and silver to reduce the quantity of the more precious metal required; and they created articles of both gold and silver by fusion, making the separate parts and then joining them together. They seem to have developed an excellent technique for achieving this; for an examination of these pieces shows that they put first gold and then silver into the mould, to create an object which was part one and part the other. They also had a method of casting ingots which were half of silver and half of gold, and it has not yet been possible to discover how they managed to keep the two metals separate along a given line.

They were also able to make metal wire, and they decorated the objects they made – in particular the ceremonial knives which are their finest creations – with circular and semicircular spangles and pendants. They used sheet metal for the knives, and the handle ended in an idol representing the feline god with all its trappings and attributes; the body was usually made up of two parts soldered together. They also used pendants in the shape of small round bells; and a common decorative theme was a chain of small spheres soldered together to form a necklace. They were skilled too in filigree work, and used turquoises as inlays, though in this latter type of work they were not always sufficiently careful: the turquoises have holes in them which show that they came from necklaces.

They also made copies in gold of the terracotta jars with double spout and bridge, which along with the ceremonial knives and some gold models of arms and hands are the finest achievements of the goldsmith's craft in Lambayeque. In addition they made ear ornaments, bracelets, necklaces of small idols and little balls, handled jars, gold figures of birds, and a great variety of vessels of all sizes, with ornamentation varying from nothing more than a rim to complicated patterns made up of reliefs on religious themes or of zoomorphic and geometric motifs.

To these treasures we must add the great masks of sheet gold representing the feline god, with projecting muzzle, almond-shaped eyes slanting upwards at the edges, and pendants hanging from its nose or mouth to represent the animal's whiskers. The most splendid of these masks usually have two gold pins in the eyes, and to each of these were fixed a ball of black resin, carefully polished, and four or five large emeralds arranged according to their size to reproduce the gleam of the creature's eyes in the dark.

In addition we find necklaces of emeralds, turquoises – ranging from light blue, the finest colour, to dark green – amethysts, lapis lazuli, pink quartz, crystalline quartz and rock crystal; and – as if this were not enough – pearls of all sizes, white, pink or black, almost always irregularly shaped, and ranging up to rather more than three-quarters of an inch in diameter.

The men of Lambayeque were skilled builders, as we can judge from the temples and fortresses of Batán Grande and the Huaca de Chotuna with their splendid friezes and the other architectural monuments in these valleys. They were also expert in cultivating the soil, and had reclaimed most of the Lambayeque valley, as their great irrigation channels show.

There was a constant cultural and commercial exchange between the men of Lambayeque and the Mochicas. Thus at Lambayeque, Pátapo, Pomalca and other sites we find tombs corresponding to the Mochica III, IV and V periods; and this culture continued to progress until it came under the control of the people of Huari.

Mochica

During the same period the Mochica culture was reaching its peak in the Chicama valley, at Santa Catalina and Virú. It is in these valleys that we find the greatest quantity of remains of the Mochica I and II periods; Mochica III, IV and V are found at Virú, Chao, Santa and Nepeña. These facts show that the Mochicas began their rise in the first two periods of the pottery classification, and that they later developed into a powerful political unit, governed by high dignitaries who directed the destinies of the kingdom and by local chiefs, as is shown in the portrait jars which have been found. Some of these jars are found throughout the country; some only in certain valleys or in limited areas within the valleys. *(Plate 96)*

The Mochicas were the leaders in a constant advance to greater achievement, until in the Mochica IV period, which produced the finest modelled pottery in ancient Peru, they reached the peak of their development – in political institutions. in religious feeling, and in intellectual achievement. They created an art of great refinement; and they also achieved refinement in the art of punishment. The punishments they inflicted were severe, though just; showing a cruelty which, it must be confessed, has been equalled by that of some nations in our own time. The punishment might take the form of cutting off the victim's nose or upper lip; but for graver offences it was more severe. The criminal's legs might be cut off, he might be exposed in the pillory, or in extreme cases put to death. The death penalty was inflicted by tying the condemned man to a tree, flaying his face so that the skin hung down over his chest like a breastplate, exposing him to be stoned by the crowd, and finally leaving him to be devoured by birds of prey. *(Plates 34, 35, 42)*

When they went to war the Mochicas wore helmets with ear-pieces which protected both sides of their face. At their belts they had ceremonial knives, hanging down either in front or behind like an appendage to their armour, and they carried shields and wooden-hafted maces with a copper head, sometimes covered with silver, slings and javelin-throwers. In battle they were accompanied by dogs who were trained to attack the enemy, and sometimes carried shields almost as tall as a man. *(Plates 38-41, 47, 52, 101, 105)*

Any enemies who were taken prisoner were exposed to ridicule, being stripped naked and made to parade in front of their captors. They were tied together by ropes round their neck and their hands were bound behind their back, while the victors wore their ornaments and weapons attached to their maces. Thereafter the prisoners, whether they were great leaders or ordinary rank and file, were destined for sacrifice: we have representations of them being thrown from cliffs or tall buildings and later being quartered. *(Plate 48)*

The Mochicas excelled both in vase-painting and in modelling: a combination which is rarely found in Peru, where the pottery tends to specialise in one or the other. The cultures of the north of Peru produced much fine work in the form of sculptured pottery, whereas in the south painted pottery was predominant; in the central part of the country the coastal cultures show both tendencies. Mochica pottery is undoubtedly the most important and the finest produced by any Peruvian culture: only the pottery of Huari, which shows a harmonious conjunction of modelling and painting, can sometimes surpass it in certain respects. The splendid modelling of the Mochica potters is seen particularly in their portrait vases, which are true works of sculpture, to be compared with the works of sculptors in other countries, and to be judged by the same standards of beauty. *(Plates 15-19)*

In these Mochica portrait jars the anatomy of the human body is subordinated to the purpose of the jar as a container. As a rule, therefore, we do not find a high standard of anatomical accuracy, and most of the jars show the crudest representation of the human body.

In their studies of the human face the Mochicas expressed all the varied moods of the human mind: laughter, tears, joy, sadness, the inward-turned glance of the blind – a whole gallery of carefully delineated psychological portraits. In these jars we can, as it were, follow their whole spiritual history. But this Mochica pottery also provides us with most valuable evidence on Peruvian prehistory. As I have said in my earlier books, it is like a three-dimensional library containing all the material we require to study this great pre-Columbian people. The Mochica pottery gives us a picture of many aspects of their life; and so it is to the cult of the dead practised by the Mochicas and other ancient peoples of Peru that we owe the abundant store of information we possess on the early inhabitants of the country.

Although the Mochica potters used only two colours – cream and red – the decoration of their work, whether consisting of geometric patterns, of scenes from everyday life covering every aspect of their existence, or of religious themes, demonstrates their remarkable skill with the brush. In their representations of human figures they do not go in for any great detail, and their pictures are drawn in a single plane, with no attempt at perspective. But the skill with which they catch the attitude of a man running, a bird flying, or fish or shellfish gliding through the water, show the progress achieved in the art of painting at this period. Although some of the pictures show a certain stiffness, others have great freedom of line, a sense of movement and of expression; and above all we can see that the artists were keen and shrewd observers of the scenes and the people they depicted. *(Plates 20, 22, 31-33, 36, 43, 57, 58, 62, 63, 65, 67-69, 114, 129)*

The Mochicas had now reached a monotheistic conception of religion. In the first three phases the feline retains its animal's head but takes on a human body. In the fourth phase it has acquired a human head, and the only traces of its animal origin are its long fangs, its wrinkled face and its whiskers. As an attribute it has a belt formed by a two-headed snake. The feline was now a deity in human form – a healer, a farmer, a fisherman. It flew through the air riding on a bird's back; it was accompanied by its faithful servant, a lizard in human shape, and a number of attendants, like the cormorant and the humming-bird; and, like man, it was accompanied everywhere by a faithful dog. *(Plates 50-51, 53)*

The feline god represented the forces of good, fighting against demons and, of course, defeating them. Among these demons we find the vampire, the crab, the snake with ears, the two-headed puma (the second head being at the place of the tail), the demon of the stones, the earth or astral demon, and the stromb or shell-fish demon. All these demons are anthropomorphic and appear in a series of paintings and sculptures representing their struggles with the feline god. In these battles the god Aia Paec was often battered and bruised; and there are representations of him being helped along by two large anthropomorphic fowls, each of them taking one of his arms.

← 53   54, 55, 56, →

57

58

62, 63, 64→

61

Aia Paec was a god who possessed the power of ubiquity and represented fruits, animals and mountains. We get an impression of his omnipotence when we find him appearing as a snail or a crab, as a duck, or in the form of maize or manioc or potatoes; and sometimes, too, we see him emerging from the topmost summit of a mountain, expressing the fact that he is also the substance of which mountains are made. *(Plates 45, 49, 54-56, 59-61)*

The Mochicas were skilled goldsmiths until the Mochica II phase; thereafter they surpassed themselves and in phases III, IV and V achieved full mastery in the art of jewellery. At this stage they were equalled only by the goldsmiths of Vicus; but since we have no evidence from tombs we cannot yet determine the date at which jewellery first appeared in ancient Peru.

The Mochicas were masters of all the arts of the goldsmith, producing work of great refinement. They did not work with gold alone but with combinations of gold and other materials, harmoniously blending gold and turquoise, amethyst and lapis lazuli, mother-of-pearl and *Spondylus pictorum* to produce delicate mosaics which were not surpassed by any pre-Hispanic civilization. Not only were ear and nose ornaments decorated with inlays of such mat erials, but whistles, pendants, necklaces, breastplates and ornaments for the forehead were enriched with a variety of materials which still further enhanced the effect of the profusion of ornament in relief. *(Plates 91, 93, 144, 147)*

These fine pieces are not, however, found in any great quantity: evidently the Mochicas' supplies of gold were smaller than those of the Lambayeque people. They were of skilled smelters and excellent coppersmiths, and they possessed the art of gilding silver. Few silver objects have survived the ravages of time, but we have enough to show that the Mochicas were also adept in the working of silver. They also knew lead and iron.

They were also magnificent architects. The Huaca del Sol, an adobe building covering more than eight hundred thousand square yards, is one of the finest monuments left by the Mochicas in the Santa Catalina valley. The Virú, Chao, Chicama and Santa valleys abound in the huge pyramidal adobe structures which formed the central point of their towns. These towns were not yet laid out on a regular plan: the inhabitants lived in huts huddled round these buildings, which were temples, palaces and fortresses in one.

The Mochicas were also skilled engineers, and their irrigation channels have never been surpassed. Working without any proper equipment, they were able to dig a canal eighty miles long, and they could divert the water of a river and convey it through the mountains to water the fields in another valley, as we can see in the canal in the Pampas de Chicama. And in the same valley they constructed an aqueduct in beaten earth, using more than two million four hundred thousand tons of earth, to irrigate thousands of acres of land and provide food for the inhabitants of the area.

Then, having occupied all the valleys, the Mochicas found themselves with no more land to cultivate and were forced to invade the pampas between the valleys by force of arms. We have evidence that they had already domesticated and cultivated the potato, the sweet potato, maize and manioc, different species of beans including *Phaseolus lunatus* and *Phaseolus vulgaris*, the *canabalia*[1], the lentil, the granadilla, the red pepper, various species of gourd, the *yacon*[2] and other plants. And this is no more than a selection from the wide range of crops they used to supply their daily food.

The Mochicas seem to have practised medicine with some degree of skill. Their pottery shows us medicine men and medicine women caring for the sick, and there are representations of Siamese twins, hare lips, cretins with club foot, and cases of leishmaniasis, leprosy, facial paralysis, exophthalmic goitre, and goitre of the neck. We also find cases of cretinism associated with goitre, tumours of the eyelids, multiple leg ulcers, tumours on the back, myxoedema, blindness due to causes which we cannot identify, glaucoma, syphilis and, probably, small-pox. The Mochica doctors also practised surgery, carrying out amputations of the nose, the lips, the arm or leg, the foot and the genital organs, practising circumcision, and carrying out skull trepanation with instruments made from sharks' teeth. They also knew the healing properties of many plants.

A people of such an advanced civilisation necessarily possessed a system of writing. The Mochicas used swift messengers, who carried their messages in small leather pouches: a service which was facilitated by the splendid network of roads covering the Mochica territory. In their pouches the messengers carried beans, on the soft part of which were inscribed messages made up of dots, parallel lines, broken lines, dots combined with straight lines, and so on. These *chasquis* (messengers) were symbolised by the falcon, the centipede and the roe-deer, while

---

[1] A perennial plant of the nettle family.   [2] *Polymnia edulis*, a sweet tuber.

those who deciphered the messages were represented by the fox, which has always been considered in the language of fable as the symbol of shrewdness and intelligence. We find representations of these beans in the pottery and the textiles at Nazca and Paracas as well as at Lambayeque. Altogether I have thousands of pieces of evidence enabling us to compare this system of writing with that of the Mayas. As we have already noted, these are the only two systems of writing in which the characters are enclosed in cartouches. Thus the Maya hieroglyphs and the Peruvian ideograms which I myself discovered have clearly a common origin. They are carved figures in the form of beans inscribed with symbols carrying various meanings. It is significant that the Maya word TZIB means "writing", and that TZ in Maya means "to draw lines" and IB "a large white bean". *(Plates 37, 44, 46)*

Space does not permit a detailed study of the civilisation of the Mochicas – their customs, their clothing, their daily life – as it is reflected in their pottery. I will note only that the lord and master of the household was the man: it was he who wore the finest jewels and the most splendid clothes. His hard-working wife meekly accepted the heaviest and most laborious tasks, looking after the children while her husband set out to conquer the neighbouring peoples for the greater glory of the Mochica kingdom.

These Indians were also a musical people, using shells as instruments of percussion, playing flutes and Pan pipes, tambourines, and straight or curved trumpets made either of pottery or of shells. With these instruments they organised orchestras to accompany their theatrical performances.

The Mochica textiles are very beautiful, with their soft colours and harmonious blending of different themes and shades. Cream seems to have been the predominant colour, though there are also a few cloths with polychrome patterns on a dark ground. These cloths show a very advanced textile technique. *(Plate 133)*

The Mochica territory is the most important centre of erotic art in America. The Mochicas, a naturally lascivious people with an exuberant imagination, enjoyed every kind of sexual pleasure; but they nevertheless recognised certain rules limiting these pleasures, and departures from the rules – for example adultery – were severely punished[1].

[1] R. LARCO HOYLE: *Checan* (Nagel, 1965).

At Virú and Chao we find the centre of the Virú culture in the Formative Epoch alongside the middle period of the Florescent Epoch. This phase contains the only examples of pottery shaped in moulds. The material is carefully selected, the firing is uniform, and the lines have gained in refinement: the spouts are more delicately shaped, the bridges are nicely rounded, and the stirrup handles are beautifully shaped and polished. Some of the jars are partly decorated with positive painting. Thus at Santa, for example, we find jars with a thick white slip covering the face of a full-length anthropomorphic figure. Other jars, of the spout-and-bridge type, show the face of a man carrying a shield, the whole thing being painted white. There are also figures of parrots in which the head and the beak are likewise painted white. In other figures the negative decoration disappears, and we find only a thick coating of kaolin slip or a positive painted decoration.

Here also we find metal-working of a high standard and large adobe buildings like those constructed by the Mochicas elsewhere. In the Santa valley, however, the Virú culture imposes its characteristics on the incised pottery and the white-on-red pottery and thus gives rise to a new culture. The roots of this culture are in the negative-decorated pottery to which I gave the name Virú, and which I discovered in the Pampa de los Cocos, in the Santa Catalina valley, some considerable time before Wendell Bennett discovered Gallinazo, as he himself recognises in one of his excellent works.-

Santa

The pottery of Santa was formerly given the name of Recuay, and later of Callejón de Huaylas; but these names are certainly wrong. The discoveries I made in the Santa valley in 1960 lead me to the conclusion that the origin of this pottery is to be sought on the coast: it is the continuation of the negative-decorated pottery of Virú. The people of Santa, who had occupied the whole of this valley, sought refuge in the mountains when the Mochicas invaded the valley during the Mochica III phase, and settled in one of the most fascinating valleys in the Peruvian Andes, the Callejón de Huaylas, lying between the two magnificently picturesque ridges of the White and the Black Cordillera. The same pottery is found also in the Chao, Virú and Nepeña valleys.

The Santa people's withdrawal into the Callejón de Huaylas did not cut them off from contact with the new occupants of the Santa valley, for the Callejón de Huaylas is merely a continuation of the Santa valley into the mountains. It is thus possible that we may find in the Callejón de Huaylas a sequence similar to that of the Santa valley. The pottery of Santa or the Callejón de Huaylas differs from that of the other cultures, but in it we find no developed forms or forms similar to those of Virú pottery. Its main distinguishing feature is that it is covered with a thick white slip, or made of pure white kaolin, or of kaolin with a pigment added to give it a pink or slightly orange tint. Most of this pottery is decorated in positive painting, but we also find negative-decorated jars showing a stylised feline figure with appendages attached to its head and nose. Thus although this culture covered its pottery with a slip it maintained the use of negative decoration into the Florescent Epoch. In this pottery the decoration is usually modelled in relief, and its special feature is that it represents not merely single figures but whole scenes – groups of figures taking part in religious ceremonies or acts of government, in festivities, or sometimes in erotic activities of religious significance.

The rather primitive simplicity of the modelling contrasts with the elaboration of the design. The expressionless faces, only summarily delineated, form a strange contrast with the variegated decoration surrounding them, which bears the mark of decadence. The composition of the scenes is simple, each one having a central figure. But the most striking feature of these works is the riot of decoration – in white, red and black – which covers the jars, expressing the overflowing sensual imagination of the artists who created them. *(Plates 75, 78, 89, 119)*

The terracotta models of buildings show unusual architectural skill. There are houses with internal courtyards, roof terraces and staircases like those found in Peru today, and houses with observation towers; and sometimes we see people in the rooms of the houses – for example a couple making love, or a woman lying naked, sunbathing.

Sometimes the decoration of the pottery has no connection with the subjects represented. Thus the animals are not shown with their characteristic markings but are covered with a complex pattern of geometric motifs – parallel lines, wavy lines, Greek key patterns or dots. As a rule the patterns are stylised. Other themes are a lizard's head, two feline heads joined within a lozenge, a two-headed snake, stylised birds' heads, and so on.

The men of Santa wore magnificent turbans in a great variety of designs; sometimes these were of considerable size, with imposing plumes of coloured feathers like those worn by the Aztecs of Mexico. They also wore large ear ornaments decorated with geometric patterns. The women wore a very simple tunic gathered in at the waist. Their necklaces were also very simple, made up of shells, lapis lazuli and quartz. The children wore necklaces of small pottery animals.

The people of Santa wore their hair shoulder-length, with a band round the forehead. Over their hair they wore a cap which covered the head-band in front and concealed the hair at the back. When the hair was allowed to grow longer it was gathered in two plaits which fell over the shoulders and breast and were fastened at the end with two large copper pins, often ornamented.

As we have noted, they were a musical people, playing the Pan pipes and the drum. The Pan pipes were not straight but oblique or stepped.

The only metal found is copper: so far there is no trace of gold or silver, or any other metal. We must remember, however, that only a small number of tombs have been discovered, and that very few of them belonged to members of the more prosperous classes of the period. We have only a few scraps of cloth to show the quality of their textiles. These demonstrate that they had already mastered the techniques of weaving and of colouring.

The dead were buried in circular pits, the bodies being usually in a seated or lying position; in a number of stone tombs, however, they are standing erect.

Here again the feline was the principal deity. It was represented with enormous teeth, sometimes in a seated position, sometimes with a semicircular knife in one hand and a trophy head in the other, and with a human head decorating its turban. In other cases we find the type of anthropomorphic feline which is common to all the cultures of the Florescent Epoch. I believe that most of the stylised patterns which cover the jars represent the feline deity, not yet in anthropomorphic form but with appendages which give it enhanced charm and symbolism.

We also discovered a number of pornographic jars, including one particularly fine example in which four women are holding a canopy over a couple engaged in sexual intercourse.

The Santa culture is one of great interest, and I have already explained my views in the brief work I wrote on this civilisation. It was unthinkable that there should be any gap in our knowledge between the Virú and the Mochica III cultures in a valley of such importance as Santa, with its splendid architectural remains. The discoveries at Santa, including not only the cemeteries but also the buildings in stone and adobe which I believe belong to a different culture, have filled this archaeological void: and they explain also how the Santa culture was able to take shape and develop with such distinctive characteristics of its own, the origin of which is undoubtedly to be sought in the civilisation of Virú.

Lima

The civilisation of Lima grew up in the central coastal area during the Florescent Epoch. Its orange-coloured pottery shows a blend – on the whole a harmonious blend – of the northern tendency towards modelling and the southern preference for painting, and we can also see clearly the influence of one of the Huari pottery types. Before this there was a stage known as "Interlocking", of which relatively few specimens are known, and this in turn derived from another earlier stage, the white-on-red pottery of the central area. *(Plate 21)*

Although I recognise that the Interlocking style is an independent decorative style, I believe that it belongs to the Lima culture. Even though this pottery has been found in isolation, it is in my opinion no more than a style of decoration. The colours used are black, white and red, and we find the same decoration applied to orange-coloured jars. As a rule the rims of these jars have the same patterns as the Lima pottery.

The large rectangular adobe buildings found at Lima – particularly those built with large adobe bricks – may belong to this culture. Those using small adobes and clay mortar belong to a later period. The pottery known as Nieveria and Cajamarquilla is attributed to the Lima culture, since it is found in the Lima valley; and this pottery is found also at Pachacamac and in the Lurín valley. Orange in colour and made from carefully selected materials, this pottery belongs to a culture of the coast; no equivalent has been found in the valleys, which have little to show in this field. We have, for all practical purposes, no material from the tombs which can be associated with the remains of buildings; nor have we any metal objects or cloth which might enable us to fill in the gaps in our knowledge. Apart from the material found by Kroeber in his excavations, we must rely entirely on the pottery for the account we can give of this civilisation.

In the pottery we find representations of human beings, animals and, above all, plants. The shapes include jars with double spout and bridge, circular vessels, jars with a narrow flat base, bottles with handles, gourd-shaped jars, sometimes with a long neck and a handle, drinking vessels with a lateral spout, globular jars with a narrow mouth and a spout, and large pots with handles on the sides.

The houses of these people had pitched roofs. They kept llamas which were used as pack animals. They cultivated gourds, beans, the *pacay*[1], peppers, squashes and tomatoes. They ate shellfish, including particularly the *spondylus*, the clam and the *pecten purpuratum*. They practised fishing, and we have a representation of a man carrying a dogfish.

This people, like other Peruvian peoples, worshipped the feline god. The god is represented in stylised animal form, accompanied by a two-headed snake which no doubt has some specific religious significance. We know that the feline was one of the most important themes treated in their pottery, and one of the most attractive in virtue of its general appearance, the colours used and the decorative treatment.

Professor Kroeber excavated some tombs at Maranga in which the bodies were wrapped in pieces of cloth or tied on to a rush litter, usually lying extended full length on their face. In some of the burials there was a single jar, in others no pottery at all.

The Florescent Epoch is of very considerable importance in the south of Peru, where it is parallel to the Mochica period. The difference between the south and the north is that the cultures of the south reach their culmination rather later than those of the north.

Paracas Pinilla
Paracas Pinilla is the continuation of Paracas Cavernas. The pottery is more refined, but the colours – which were applied after firing between the incised areas – are less durable than those of Paracas Cavernas. The colours tend towards pastel shades and are very skilfully blended to produce an attractive effect. As at Paracas Cavernas, the patches of colour are separated by areas patterned in incised lines, but here the incised areas are smaller and the figures slenderer and more delicate.

[1] A fruit tree, *Enga Feuillei*.

Radiocarbon dating gives us a date of 307 B.C., plus or minus 200 years. Other investigations suggest a date about A.D. 2000. I myself would favour a compromise solution and would put Paracas Necrópolis in the early phase of the Florescent Epoch.

Paracas Necrópolis
Here I found some red jars with imperfectly finished spouts, rather longer than the spouts of the pottery usually attributed to Nazca, and decorated with Nazca motifs in white. These jars were rather primitive in character, and I classified them as "Ica white-on-red". Since very few of them were known I felt compelled to make a fuller study of the south of Peru, and reached the conclusion that these jars were not the ones I was looking for. This supported the hypothesis I had already formed, namely that the white-on-red pottery of this area is the pottery type known as Paracas Necrópolis. Here we found red jars and jars with a white slip like those of Salinar and Vicus, as well as jars with white-on-red decoration.

The same phenomenon occurred in the south of Peru as we have already noted in the north. At the end of the Formative Epoch in the north the Cupisnique art of modelling disappears suddenly and a new culture appears, with pottery which shows an improvement in technique but a sharp decline in modelling skill. Over all, the art of the period is inferior to what had gone before. In the south the incised and painted pottery of Paracas attains its peak with the Pinilla jars, which are almost covered with patterns marked out by incised lines, as we have already noted, and splendidly painted in many colours; but when we come to Paracas Necrópolis, which is similar to Salinar, this style disappears almost overnight. The incised and painted pottery gives place to a series of beautifully shaped jars, often with delicate spouts, but in a uniform terracotta red. In a very few exceptional cases the jars are white, decorated with simple geometric patterns in red.

It is clear that these cultures characterised by white-on-red pottery arose at a time of artistic decline throughout Peru. Both sculpture and painting deteriorated and did not recover until the vigorous upsurge of the Florescent Epoch.

We already knew the beginnings of positive decoration in this type of pottery, following the stage marked by the painting of areas marked out by incised lines – for example after the transitional Cupisnique period; and of course we also knew the negative-painted jars from the burials in the caves. We were also aware of the stage at which positive decoration was partly superseded by negative decoration. Clearly, therefore, the development of art in the south had followed the same course as in the north. We were thus concerned with three decorative styles which had passed through the same metamorphoses and transformations as in the north, but on pottery of different types from those found in northern Peru.

All these elements, together with a new element – the art of polychrome painting of pottery – contributed to the formation of the Nazca culture, by way of a stage which in my classification is the stage of development from Paracas to Nazca. The pottery consists of jars with incised decoration, painted before firing. Positive painted motifs gradually became general on jars with polychrome painting like those of Paracas; but in the Nazca pottery the motifs are not marked out by incised lines but with the brush, in a natural development of the positive painting technique.

The Paracas Necrópolis culture was discovered by Dr Tello at Cerro Colorado. The cemeteries consisted of large enclosures, within which were smaller enclosures; and inside these, packed closely together, were found a considerable number of conical "mummy bundles". The bodies within the bundles were in a sitting position, with their knees drawn up against their chests, their heads resting on their knees and their arms tied to their sides. The embalmed bodies were on wicker baskets, which in turn rested on rush mats, and were found in an excellent state of preservation. They were wrapped in lengths of undecorated cloth, wound round the mummified body so as to give it a conical shape. Within these wrappings were a variety of funerary offerings, along with splendid garments and the marvellous Paracas cloaks, which are unequalled anywhere in the world for the beauty of their patterns and their colouring. The cloth used is cotton, or wool, or a mixture of both. The designers were great artists, men of daring imagination, who composed their patterns with such skill that from a combination of different and clashing colours they were able to achieve a magnificent harmony. The Paracas cloaks, along with those of Chanca, are probably the finest examples of textiles to be found anywhere in the world. And these Indians were equally skilled in all the techniques for producing and decorating cloth, from knitting to embroidery.

Inside the mummy bundles we usually find the mummy wearing a splendid turban, surrounded by the funerary offerings. From them we can learn a great deal about the people of this period. Their clothing consisted of a short sleeved shirt, a loincloth, a small skirt or kilt, a large cloak worn over the shoulders, and the magnificent turban already mentioned. They might adorn themselves, too, with fox skins and knitted caps. They were fond of wearing turbans rolled round their head, and in particular a type similar to the *llautos* worn by the Incas. They were able to make rope, and could make bags. To cool themselves they used large fans made from the feathers of condors, macaws or other birds, carefully woven into a fabric of rushes. They also used feathers for the decorative plumes which they wore on their heads. They knew the use of needles.

The people of Paracas Necrópolis cultivated cotton, maize, manioc, canna, groundnuts, squashes, the Lima bean and various species of small beans.

When they went to war they used lances, large javelins with obsidian points, pointed bone instruments, and stone maces with wooden hafts. Their great chieftains carried sceptres of carved wood; some of them decked themselves with necklaces of *spondylus* shells, or wore ornaments of sheet gold on their garments or their turban. They played bone flutes with four vents and Pan pipes, also made of bone.

Because of the gold found in these tombs and the very advanced textile techniques I have classified this culture in the Florescent Epoch and not, as I ought to have done, at the end of the Formative Epoch. As I have already suggested, however, the cultures of the southern coastal area seem to have been relatively backward and to have reached their full flowering only in the middle and late phases of the Florescent Epoch.

We cannot draw any useful conclusions about the architecture, for no pottery has been found associated with the buildings. The pottery itself shows simple lines, sometimes with delicate Greek key patterns incised on it; usually it is painted in a single colour or in two colours, using no motifs that call for particular mention. The cultures of the south paid much more attention to painting than those of the north, and the white slip and the red paint are much thicker than in the north. We find representations of fruits, of lizards, of ducks, and of other birds which it is difficult to identify. I have seen a single jar with a figure of a reclining feline.

The textiles, on the other hand, tell us the whole history of this people. The ancient inhabitants of Paracas have left us in these splendid materials an immense range of pictures of their daily life, the description of which would fill many volumes.

In them we find representations of the feline deity and its retinue, of great chieftains wearing all the garments which have been found in the tombs, of warriors, of women, of all the birds of the region, of people carrying fruit in their hands. For the purposes of our present study, however, the most important feature is that the feline deity is now given human form in a finely stylised representation: it has a long tongue in the form of a snake and brandishes batons or sceptres ending in a snake's head. There are also jars containing beans of different colours, and cloaks with borders containing thousands of ideographic signs; for the people of Nazca and Paracas used colours as well as symbolic lines in their ideograms and thus greatly increased the richness of their script.

Much has been written about the technique of mummification used at Paracas. Examination shows that the bodies and the cloaks are impregnated with an acrid liquid, which may have been deliberately applied to the mummy bundles in order to preserve the contents. Some people are allergic to the Paracas cloaks, finding that handling them produces an itching of the skin and sometimes a swelling of the hands.

The people of Paracas practised skull deformation, beginning in childhood. They used the method known as annular deformation, producing a vertical elongation of the skull so that the ears seem to be brought back towards the posterior part of the head. This deformation caused grave damage to the bony structure, leading in particular to osteoporosis. A few trepanned skulls have been found, but I believe that most of the large perforations that have been noted are the result of disease rather than trepanation. The uneven thickness of the edges of these perforations is due to the fact that the external surface was more severely attacked than the internal.

It is interesting to note that the pottery of this culture is without ornamentation, their skill in ornamentation being concentrated on their textiles. The south of Peru shows an interesting development: first we find, both at Paracas Cavernas and Paracas Pinilla, jars covered with ornamental patterns in many colours, and this is followed by the Necrópolis phase in which the pottery consists of a few gourds and of jars with refined geometrical shapes but no ornamentation at all.

Thus at Cavernas and Pinilla the art of textiles is predominant over the art of pottery, and the artists' decorative skill is transferred from jars and vases to cloaks. Later, at Nazca, pottery was again to achieve the pre-eminence, and the surface of the jars was covered with magnificent polychrome designs. We find the same phenomenon in the north, where the art of modelling which achieved such energy and beauty in the Cupisnique culture was superseded by a new style, which admittedly – as at Paracas Cavernas – showed an improvement in ceramic technique but also – as at Salinar – a decline in modelling skill: a skill which was later to reappear with renewed vigour in the orange ware and to reach its highest point with the Mochicas.

Throughout almost the whole of the southern coastal area of Peru we observe that the decorative patterns used on pottery are for the most part textile patterns. In other words, as we have already noted, the art of textiles has achieved predominance over the art of pottery; and as a result this art of the south has not the strength and virility of the art of the north. It is, I think, a feminine art, reflecting the delicate touch of the women who wove the cloths; and we may reasonably suppose that the potters who produced this delicately fashioned pottery were also women.

According to Yacovleff four hundred and twenty-nine mummy bundles were found in 1927 on the northern slopes of the Cerro Colorado. We may hope, therefore, that when the excavations are completed they will unlock many of the secrets of this culture which are still undecipherable. It is a very great pity that so little pottery has survived: only a few pieces have been found, associated with javelins made of wood or of reeds.

We now come to the Nazca culture of the Florescent Epoch on the south coast; and here I follow the classification laid down by Dr. Alfred Kroeber, to whose teaching I owe so much.

Nazca A
This is the name given by Dr. Kroeber to the simple naturalistic pottery, painted in many colours, which is found in the valleys of Pisco, Chincha, Ica, Nazca, Palpa and Acari in the southern coastal area of Peru. In this polychrome pottery modelling now takes second place: the figures are very roughly shaped, and achieve their effect from the complex pattern of colours with which they are covered. As in all Peruvian pottery, we find jars in the shape of human beings, animals, plants and so on; but most of them are decorated with delicately drawn patterns, richly coloured. The forms, of course, are different from those found in

the northern and central areas: the southern types begin at Paracas, as we have already seen, and we can perhaps find the first intimations at Vicus in the Department of Piura. The commonest forms are jars with small double spouts and a bridge, elongated jars, flat dishes, vessels in the shape of a truncated cone, and round jars with a spout. We find also painted portrait jars and simple anthropomorphic jars with a spout on top. There is a wide variety of decoration: trophy heads, birds, complicated geometrical patterns, figures of people engaged in various activities, mammals, fish and reptiles, all drawn with exquisite taste. The animals are represented with great naturalness, eating, swimming, or standing still; and the same naturalness is shown in the other scenes, and in the simple ornamentation. *(Plate 15)*

The anthropomorphic jars show the people of Nazca pursuing two activities, agriculture and fishing. We see the fishermen with their nets and the farmers carrying the vegetables which provided them with food. Among cultivated plants we find canna, peppers, beans, cactuses, cucumbers and some of the *sapotaceae. (Plates 80, 111)*

The swallow and the humming-bird are favourite subjects, and we also find the toucan, the condor, and other sea-birds and birds of prey, all represented with great beauty and delicacy. There are also many representations of fish, covering practically every variety found off the coasts of Peru. *(Plate 115)*

There are also figures of warriors armed with very simple weapons.

The representations of religious subjects are of particular importance. Large numbers of jars have figures of the anthropomorphic feline deity, showing the influence of the Paracas type, but nevertheless representing a new conception of the supreme being. This is no longer Aia Paec in a simplified representation of the human shape, but a deity with a long tail which ends in a head, in a splendid stylisation on which the artists have lavished all the resources of their art. Basically, however, this deity, like Aia Paec, is the anthropomorphic feline. It has a human face with feline whiskers; and in some cases the whiskers form part of a gold mask which covers the mouth or curls up in a semicircle on either side of the nose. The feline god also wears head ornaments, some of which we found among the funerary offerings in the tombs. Its ears are shown on top of its head or, more usually, on each side of its face. Sometimes, too, we find the feline god transformed into a bird, or into a centipede, or into a profusion of fruit which springs from his body; for this god, like the god of the Mochicas, had the gift of ubiquity and the power to transform himself into different shapes, since it was he who gave life to the whole of nature. *(Plate 108)*

There were also demons like the sperm whale, which is represented brandishing in one hand a human head, held by the hair, and in the other a semicircular knife. *(Plate 21)*

The geometric ornament is simple. A number of different types can be distinguished: cream-coloured jars with a simple black pattern, jars with red decoration on a cream base, and jars decorated only with a cream slip.

From the technical point of view the textiles of Nazca are not inferior to those of Paracas, but they are on an altogether lower level of excellence, and we do not find at Nazca anything comparable to the splendidly coloured garments of Paracas.

Metal-working in Nazca was still in its infancy compared with the northern coastal area. Objects in sheet metal are usually of poor workmanship, and the repoussé work is even worse. The articles found comprise a few breastplates, large nose ornaments like those sometimes worn by the feline deity, and long pins in the form of a bird. As we have noted in relation to other similar objects, these are all of religious significance. Most of the nose ornaments are decorated with representations of snakes. We also find head ornaments and necklaces of gold, turquoise, lapis lazuli and shells.

We cannot say anything definite about Nazca architecture. So far it has not been possible to associate the various types of pottery found in these valleys with the surviving remains of buildings. Most of the burials were in irregularly shaped pits, but there are also some tombs with walls of round adobe bricks and a roof formed of carob logs. The bodies are usually in a flexed position.

In marked contrast with the delicate small-scale decoration and the poor modelling of the Nazca pottery are the monumental zoomorphic sculptures with geometric ornament which we find in the sandy area between Nazca and Palpa. We cannot determine whether these objects belong to Nazca A, Chanca or Nazca B: all that we can say is that monumental sculpture similar to this is found in the north of

Peru. On a low hill near Chimbote is an enormous snake built of stones piled on top of one another, with its body winding downhill and its head on the level of the plain. Monumental sculpture of this kind is also found in other parts of Peru.

The people of Nazca do not seem to have been warlike, though many spear-throwers and javelins tipped with obsidian have been found in the tombs.

Chanca

At the time when Nazca A was at its peak we find a new culture appearing in these southern valleys – a culture related to another which probably originated in the mountains. This is suggested by the discovery of Chanca pottery in all the valleys where the Nazca culture flourished. The pottery of Nazca was strongly influenced by this pottery, which brought with it new themes and new forms. And this pottery in turn seems to have taken something from the typical Nazca and Paracas forms, for in it we find jars with double spout and bridge, modelled jars with spout and bridge, elongated jars and other forms which are usually to be related to Nazca pottery.

This pottery has usually a dark beige or brick-red base, but there are also jars with a black or lead-coloured base. A distinctive feature of the representations of human figures is their slanting semicircular eyes. The decorative themes are no longer strictly figurative: they tend now to be idealised, and geometrical patterns have become more important. The decoration has one curious characteristic – the long lines ending in a hook which enclose the main decorative themes. These themes are sometimes geometric; sometimes they consist of ideograms; sometimes they are of religious significance. But the principal innovation we find in this culture is the scenes painted on some of the jars. Most of these are scenes of war or hunting. Taken along with the frequent representations of men armed with spear-throwers, javelins or other weapons, this suggests that this people was of a warlike nature and eager for conquest. *(Plate 18)*

In addition to the typical pottery forms we find bottles with handles, lenticular vessels with a single spout and a handle, globular jars with a wide mouth, and large numbers of globular vessels with necks in the form of a human face. There are also pots of rectangular section and double jars with spout and bridge.

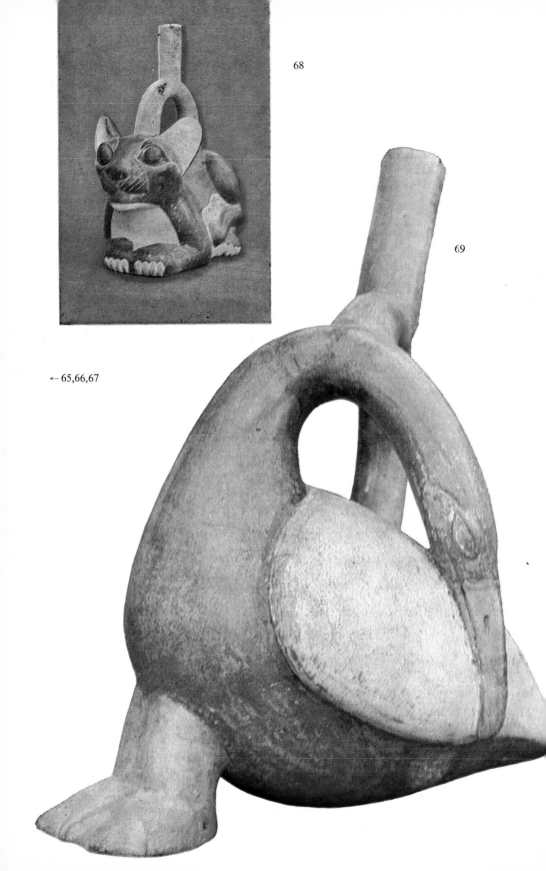

68

← 65,66,67

69

70

72
73 →
74

71

←75

7●

77

79, 80

82

83

84

85

86

88

89, 90
91, 92 →

96

97

In the pottery of this culture, unlike that of other cultures, we frequently find representations of women, including exquisitely modelled figures of naked women. These are found also in Nazca pottery. *(Plates 83, 131)*

The textile art of the Chancas shows that in this respect too they had achieved a high level of civilisation. The cloaks preserved in the Rafael Larco Herrera Museum and in some foreign museums are equal to the best Paracas products. Evidently the people of Chanca, like all the peoples of the Florescent Epoch in the Department of Ica, were masters of textile design and production. They had the advantage of having access to supplies of cotton, which was used on a large scale, as it still is today. In the north of Peru, on the other hand, it has only become possible quite recently to grow cotton, following the discovery of powerful insecticides to deal with the pests to which it is subject. With favourable conditions for the growing of its main raw material, textile production in southern Peru was able to make rapid strides. In this part of the country it was possible to achieve proper selection of varieties so as to obtain the best fibres, and thus improve considerably on the brown cotton which is still found growing wild in the north of Peru. It is only in this way that we can explain the high quality of the raw material used in southern Peru. There is no doubt – as I have been able to satisfy myself by personal observation – that the fine threads employed were derived from selected fibres

These peoples of southern Peru also had the advantage of living near the areas which produced llama, alpaca and vicuña wool, in what are now the Departments of Cuzco and Puno and others in southern and central Peru.

This culture had a profound influence, particularly on the art of decoration, introducing new elements which put an end to the simplicity of the realistic and naturalistic art of the Nazca culture. The decoration was overloaded with a series of extraneous elements which complicated the pattern, like the hooked lines which have already been mentioned.

The Chanca people knew the use of gold. The Tello collection contains a splendid circular plaque of sheet gold, with representations in repoussé of the feline god.

Their tombs were small enclosures of earth or clay, built of adobe bricks, semi-circular in shape and roofed, like the Nazca tombs, with carob logs. According to Tello the heads were deformed from front to rear (fronto-occipital deformation), showing a variation in practice from the frontal deformation usually practised at Nazca.

133

The weapons used by the Chanca people included lances, feathered maces and javelins.

We shall not to be able to discuss Chanca architecture until Dr. Tello, who has excavated more than five hundred Nazca and Chanca tombs in this area, has published the results of his investigations.

Nazca B

The result of Chanca influence on the simple naturalistic pottery of Nazca A was to produce a flamboyant decorative style in which ornament proliferated and the jars were covered with a riot of decoration which has a distinctly decadent effect. This rococo style is known as Nazca B.

In this new style the decorative pattern is complicated by the use of hooked lines or lines in the shape of a harpoon with several points. We can also see Chanca influence in the shapes of the pottery. In addition to portrait jars, depicting yellowish faces with semicircular eyes, there are a great variety of different shapes, including globular vessels, vessels in the shape of a truncated cone, and jars with double spout and bridge. The head-shaped jars with a spout and handles which are common in the Nazca A phase are now much less frequently found; and this too is a feature of the Chanca culture. During this phase, also, there is a marked change in the shape of the jars: they are not cylindrical but almost always have a cleft either in the middle of the jar or near the opening. There is an increase in the number of bell-shaped jars and of globular vessels with a large mouth which is wider than the vessel itself. The forms are more or less uniform in the Chanca and Nazca B styles, except that the flat dish-shaped type of vessel is rarely found in Nazca B. It would also be fair to say that in general, though the same forms persist, the proportions of the different types vary. *(Plates 14, 82)*

Nazca B took over the anthropomcrphic and zoomorphic figures of the Chanca pottery and, as we have already seen, it also inherited from Chanca a whole series of decorative elements – religious motifs, abstract patterns, human figures, and parts of humans and animals, stylised or idealised – as well as a range of colours including red, orange, beige, white and grey. We still find the feline god, but it is now exaggeratedly stylised by the addition of these various decorative elements. Sometimes we find ornamental motifs similar to those on the Raimondi stele from the Chavín temple. Representations of the feline as such are more rarely found, but parts of the feline's body are commonly found in stylised form, in a pattern of lines and hooks.

The feline always wears an ornament which is not quite a nose ornament, nor a lip ornament, nor a breastplate, but a combination of all three. It was usually made of sheet gold, and was placed over the creature's muzzle, with an aperture at the position of the mouth. The lower part came down to the breast, and at the lower ends were two appendages representing the whiskers; sometimes these ended in snakes' heads. In the upper part there were two pieces pointing up towards the nose, and sometimes two other pieces curling round the eyes.

This culture was contemporary with the Mochica III phase, and this confirms my theory that the Chavín temple was also contemporary with Mochica III, corresponding to the middle period of the Florescent Epoch. These elements are not found in the Formative Epoch. As some archaeologists have already recognised, the Nazca B style may well have had some influence on the religious art in the Chavín temple.

About Nazca B architecture we have no concrete information; and we have little detailed knowledge of their metal-working techniques.

Representations of plants are rare. There are some representations of cucumbers, but no other fruits or vegetables have been identified.

Of Nazca B textiles, as of Nazca A, we have very few examples, though there are some very fine specimens with decorations on religious themes. The Paracas, Nazca A and B, and Chanca textiles form a unity which extends from the Formative to the Florescent Epoch of the civilisations of southern Peru. In pottery we find the following forms, already observed at Vicus, and many of them also at Virú and Salinar: zoomorphic spout-and-bridge vessels, globular spout-and-bridge vessels in the form of a human or animal head or body, and globular vessels with a sloping spout on one side and a flattened bridge running from the spout to the other side. We also find the double jars with spout and bridge which are so common at Rukana and Huari, and forms derived from them. In my investigations at Vicus I discovered a falcon – now in the Rafael Larco Herrera Museum – with a flattened spout and bridge and with incised lines, which but for its terracotta colour might be taken for a transitional form from Paracas or Nazca. The curious thing is that we do not find in this culture the elongated jars or the flat dish forms which are so common in the civilisations of the south. *(Plates 85, 90)*

For all these reasons, and also because stirrup-spouted jars have been found both at Paracas and at Chanca, I am convinced that the north exerted a strong cultural influence on the south. It must be borne in mind also that the religious ideas of the ancient Peruvians, in particular the gradual transformation of the feline into a humanised deity, developed simultaneously not only along the whole coastline of Peru but also in the mountains. And it is worth repeating also that the system of writing found on the Mochica painted pottery also appears on the Paracas cloaks, the textiles of Nazca and the pottery of Pukara – in other words, from one end of Peruvian territory to the other.

Cajamarca

The main centre of the pottery called Cajamarca, to which Tello gave the name Marañón, is in the Department of Cajamarca. This type of pottery extends into the Amazon area, into the mountains in the Department of La Libertad, and to the north of Ancash. Occasional pieces have been found which had travelled as far as the coastal area, to Piura, Trujillo and Lambayeque. Since the Department of Lambayeque borders on the Department of Cajamarca, it was there that the influence of this culture was most strongly felt.

The pottery of Cajamarca is light orange in colour, or occasionally cream. Two clearly distinguishable types are found: one with polychrome decoration covering the whole of the jar, the other with simple geometric patterns, usually in two colours, covering only part of the surface. The zoomorphic designs are mostly stylised. The decoration is characterised by the use of very small motifs arranged in circles or in lines or marked out by parallel broken lines. The potters preferred to cover the whole surface of the jar. In some cases the decoration is applied to the inside, and the outside has practically no decoration; in others the main decoration is on the outside and the inner surface has only a pattern of parallel lines running across each other or a stylised representation of an animal.

The principal pottery forms are tripod jars, stemmed vessels and cups in the shape of a truncated cone, lenticular vessels with small lateral handles on the sides, globular amphoras with small lateral handles and small flared necks, and globular urns standing on a base. These urns have a very large mouth, sometimes wider than the lower part, and have a small handle with which to hold the urn while drinking. There are also some zoomorphic jars with necks, showing very primitive modelling, and decorated spoons.

136

The decoration of some jars is similar to certain types found in Costa Rica. In general the people of this civilisation seem to have concentrated all their spiritual and intellectual resources on the profusion of decoration which covers their pottery. The colour is usually cream with a slight tinge of orange, with the design painted in brick-red; but there are some jars which are half orange and half light grey, others with red or beige designs on a beige base, and others again with patterns in black and orange. Geometric motifs are common. The zoomorphic figures are highly stylised and ornamented with representations of snakes, reptiles' heads and felines, in a style completely different from anything else found in Peru. In spite of its highly developed stylisation it is a style very easy to recognise. The jars are usually divided into sections with separate decorative patterns: thus we find a jar of truncated cone shape divided into a circular band round the base with its own ornamental motif, four trapezoidal sections on the sides and an edging of geometric motifs like volutes and concentric circles.

The occurrence of representations of the feline on the pottery of Cajamarca does not give us sufficient material to discuss the religion of this people.

This, in brief, is all we know of the Cajamarca culture. In spite of the great quantity of pottery that has been found and its wide spread, our information is in fact disappointingly incomplete.

Pallasca
At Pallasca, in the Department of Ancash, we found a few monoliths, some sculptured figures of the feline, and a number of stelae, similar to those found at Callejón de Huaylas and Cajamarca. There seems to have been a strong Mochica influence on this culture, for on some of the monoliths we find the characteristic Mochica mutilated heads. Moreover the geometric elements and the stylisation of the feline are similar to the Mochica style.

This culture extends as far as the Department of La Libertad. Max Uhle found sculptures at Marca Huamachuco similar to those I have described. McCown carried out excavations in this area and found pottery of Cajamarca, North Huari A, North Huari B, Santa and Inca types. He also found other types of pottery, so that it is not possible to associate the pottery with the monumental buildings of this great pre-Columbian city. And I have seen only a few photographs of jars found at Pallasca which show very definite Mochica influence.

Callejón de Huaylas

The pottery known as Recuay was formerly thought to correspond to the culture of Callejón de Huaylas, though this pottery was never found in association with any of the thousands of monoliths, stelae and other sculptured stones which are found all over the Callejón de Huaylas and show a similarity of technique which indicates that they belong to a single culture. We have already described, under the name of Santa, the pottery which was formerly known as Callejón de Huaylas. There must, however, have existed in this paradisiac valley a culture to which these sculptures are to be attributed, for they are associated not only with buildings constructed from field stones supported by smaller stones but with splendid sarcophagi made from a single block of stone with a cover slab which is carefully dressed and polished. There must, therefore, have been earlier cultures here before the arrival of the people of Santa.

Chavín

The Chavín temple is one of the most important religious centres to be found in the Andes. The indigenous peoples of Peru believed that the feline god lived in some remote mountain area, and this idea is realistically expressed in the Mochica sculptures, which show the feline amid mountains represented by jutting points. All along the Andes we find a series of temples of the greatest importance, such as Pacopampa, Kuntur Wasi, Marca Huamachuco, Chavín, Huari, Pukara and Tiahuanaco. The finest of these, however, is the temple of Chavín de Huantar. It is a magnificent building constructed of rectangular stones carefully polished and worked like rectangular adobes, with staircases, columns carved by skilled sculptors, and walls decorated with stone slabs representing snakes, human heads, and felines. The carvings, rather reminiscent of Gothic gargoyles, show great skill in stylisation and a lively imagination applied to religious themes. The temple is of solid masonry and does not contain any large rooms; it has a series of passages, like those of the Pacopampa temple, and a small sanctuary in the centre containing the great Chavín stele representing the feline god in all his majesty. *(Plates 149, 166)*

I have previously suggested, and I still maintain, that the Chavín temple was erected by the people of Nepeña. Chavín was not a cultural centre, still less the capital of a large people; and moreover I believe that the Chavín temple belongs to the Florescent and not the Formative Epoch. Chavín represents the culmination of the art of incised decoration, which arose during the Formative Epoch and achieved its finest flowering in this area. Those who maintain that the Chavín temple is to be dated to the Formative Epoch, along with Sechín, Cupisnique, Punkurí and other buildings of the same period, are in my view grossly in error. We have only to compare the beauty of form of the carvings on the stelae and columns at Chavín, and on the Raimondi stele in particular, with the Sechín bas-reliefs and the modelled pottery and small sculptured stones of Cupisnique, Pacopampa or Kuntur Wasi to realise that these are two quite separate styles, many centuries apart. The sculptures of the latter type belong to the very infancy of art; those of the Chavín temple show an art in the fullness of its aesthetic achievement.

The Chavín carvings are in a characteristic style which I have called banded relief. They seem almost to have been drawn with ruler and compasses, so regular are the curves and so exactly parallel the straight lines; and this gives them a dynamic rhythm and a beauty of their own. With the help of this technique the artists of Chavín were able to perfect still further the figures of the mythical beings which they depicted. We find the same style producing equally beautiful results in the pottery of the Mochica III period. As I have already noted, there is a connection between the polychrome decoration and the ornamental hooked lines of Nazca B and the representation of the feline god on the Raimondi stele.

Chavín belongs, therefore, to the Florescent Epoch, as do Cerro Blanco and Mojeque, which are of the same period. The Rafael Larco Herrera Museum contains two jars of exceptional quality which, according to the illustrious and reverend Director of the Huaraz Museum, Augusto Soriano Infante, were found in the Chavín temple. One of them is a conical cup, the other a vessel of elongated globular shape with a thin stirrup spout and a lip similar to the type found in the Mochica I period. Both jars have incised decoration. They are not fired black like those of the Formative Epoch, but are covered with a black slip, in the manner characteristic of the Florescent Epoch.

A discovery of great importance was made in the Chavín temple, in the form of some fragments of Mochica pottery. The temple must have been a veritable Mecca to the worshippers of the feline god, frequented by pilgrims from many different cultures. I believe, therefore, that Chavín was not a culture in its own right, but one of the elements in a culture which flourished in the Florescent Epoch. It is a profound error to regard Chavín as a great cultural centre, when it is in reality merely a consequence of the flowering of a decorative style of the Formative Epoch.

Perhaps I may conclude this digression by stressing that these errors can be attributed to the fact that there has so far been no detailed study of the Chavín temple and the stelae found in its neighbourhood.

Any art critic could see at once the difference between the incised religious style of the Formative Epoch and the style found in the Chavín temple. What is now required is a programme of investigations directed to establishing the various phases of this decorative style, which my own work has enabled me to classify and date correctly.

Huari

One of the most important civilisations in Peru grew up round Ayacucho and achieved a considerable spread, for its pottery is found from Huancayo to Huanta and Huancavelica. This pottery used to be known as Tiahuanaco or Tiahuanacoid: a serious misnomer, for the centre of this culture was not on the high plateau but in the territory of the Wankas. This was the theory I expounded to my unforgettable friend Wendell Bennett, and this was what brought him to Huari after the Virú expedition. The pottery found at Conchopata shows the variety of pottery types belonging to the various phases of this culture, which have been studied both by Peruvian and North American archaeologists.

There can be no doubt that the various phases of Huari exerted an influence, not only in the Epoch of Fusion but also in the Florescent Epoch, on the cultures of Lima and Ica – i.e., Nazca, Chanca and Nazca B. The largest finds of sherds have been at Conchopata, near Ayacucho, and Pacheco in the Ica valley. On both sites pottery of similar types was found, and in particular the so-called monumental pottery – jars much larger in size than those of any other culture, with the exception of the large aryballi of Cuzco and a few bell-shaped jars of the Mochica culture.

The Huari pottery of Ayacucho relies both on modelling and on colour for its decoration. The National Museum contains a large number of jars which have been put together from fragments found at Pacheco and at Kawachi in the Nazca valley. These include large cups decorated both internally and externally with religious themes, human figures being associated with plants in the decorative pattern. *(Plates 106, 116)*

There are also some finely shaped amphoras with a large neck on which is a perfectly modelled head. The head is usually dark red in colour, and the face may be painted. On the sides of the jars are two hands emerging from the handles. There are also jars with representations of llamas, and double jars in the form of faces. All this pottery belongs to the Huari culture and probably all came from the same area but was transported to the coast.

In this pottery we find the polychrome chevron which is the main decorative theme of the Huari culture. The smaller vessels include all the types which later, in the Epoch of Fusion, were to spread throughout the whole of Peru.

The ruins of Huari shows that there were populous centres in this culture. In some areas we find two types of building superimposed. The lower parts, belonging to the Florescent Epoch of the Huari culture, are built of dressed stone, usually in rectangular blocks, while the upper parts are built of field stones of uniform size, laid closely together. The walls were decorated with sculptured slabs representing the heads of felines.

We also find at Huari monumental sculpture in stone, in the form of statues intended for the adornment of temples. These represent figures of men and of women with splendid coiffures which are reproduced with great naturalism. These works show striking progress in the art of stone sculpture. In addition to these large statues, however, the Huari culture produced also little statuettes in turquoise, which were at first confined to this area but later spread throughout Peru at the time of the Huari expansion. These exquisite little figures show the most delicate craftsmanship. They normally range in size from 3 to 4 inches high; the smallest are little more than half an inch high. They are similar in form to the globular jars with human heads which have already been mentioned in the section on pottery. They differ considerably in the dress worn by the figures. *(Plate 123)*

The people of Huari were also skilled metal-workers. In the Rafael Larco Herrera Museum we possess a copper figure of an anthropomorphic feline, which was given to the author of this work by Dr. Wendell Bennett after his excavations at Huari. There are also beautifully worked gold masks; and I can recall a large turban with crescent-shaped spangles, and gold plates with a representation of the feline's head, which no doubt were intended for the decoration of turbans.

At Huari itself there are stone-built tombs, and we also find stone sarcophagi superimposed on one another. There are also common graves, no doubt for the poorer people who could not afford any better means of burial.

This splendid culture developed at the same pace as the other cultures of Peru from the Formative Epoch onwards, as is shown by the finding of incised pottery near Huancayo and at other points in Huari territory. Then the Huari people, having risen to importance, felt strong enough to set out to conquer Peru towards the end of the Florescent Epoch. Scattered throughout the country we find cemeteries with Huari burials, containing pottery and offerings belonging to the same culture. It is clear, therefore, that we are not concerned here with a purely cultural influence or with the spread of a particular type of Andean pottery but with a conquest in the full sense of the term.

We then find a period of predominance of Huari art, followed by the creation of a hybrid style produced by the mingling of Huari culture with the culture of the conquered people. It is at this period that we see the beginnings of Andean art, based on a fusion between the cultures of the coast and the other parts of the Andes area. From the time of the Huari invasion the various cultures which developed in the Formative and Florescent Epochs began to lose their original purity, and in the cultures which were conquered by the mountain peoples we now find an Andean element.

Pukara

At Pukara, in the province of Lampa and the Department of Puno, a type of pottery has been found which differs from the pottery of the other cultures but is related to the pottery of Tiahuanaco. This culture was first described by Dr. Luis E. Valcárcel in 1925. Of the pottery practically nothing survives but fragments. In the Rafael Larco Herrera Museum we have only one small complete vessel, and the National Museum contains two, both of them broken. Apart from these we have nothing but sherds. What we have, however, tell us something about the Pukara pottery, which possesses individual characteristics distinguishing it from other cultures and is among the most highly prized for its beauty. It is incised and painted, the colour being applied before firing, and has been highly polished to produce a remarkably fine finish. The people of Pukara were masters of sculpture and modelling, and must certainly be dated to the Florescent rather than the

Formative Epoch. Although they used incised lines to mark out the decorated areas this later dating is clearly established by the excellent firing and the progress shown in modelling and painting skill.

It is difficult to discuss the shapes of the pottery since we must depend on reconstructions which may often be works of pure imagination. The small vessels which I have seen are of inverted trapezoidal form, and there are also rectangular jars, jars in truncated cone shape, and flat dishes. From the fragments I have examined it is possible to deduce that there were many cup-shaped vessels and many conical ones. The decoration is painted in either red or cream. The motifs include human faces and representations of the feline, sometimes in a magnificent anthropomorphic version. There are also figures of birds like the condor, and scenes showing people leading animals by a halter or human or animal figures brandishing a sceptre similar to those found at Tiahuanaco. Most of the ornamental motifs, however, are geometric – lozenges, stepped lines, Greek key patterns and permutations and combinations of these themes.

We also find at Pukara buildings belonging to the same culture, constructed of large polished rectangular blocks of dressed stone. The remains show a considerable degree of architectural skill in achieving a regular layout with rectangular or semicircular rooms separated by corridors and entered by doorways opening on these corridors. The rectangular blocks in the walls were built up to produce an effect similar to adobe.

The Pukara people were also skilled in monumental sculpture, in a style similar to that of Tiahuanaco. We find, for example, a tall figure of an anthropomorphic feline, with large round eyes, carrying in his hands a human head and a large implement which is probaly a *tumi* (a semicircular knife). In addition there are human figures with a skeleton-like body showing the ribs exposed, and stelae – again similar to some sculptures found at Tiahuanaco – showing the full-length figure of a feline with stylised geometric patterns round its head. But we also find stelae in a completely different style, like the Sarapa stele or the one decorated with symbolic figures in a highly refined geometric style not found in any other area in the Andes. The main theme of these stelae is a fish, thought by local people to represent the *suche* found in Lake Titicaca. We also find sculptures decorated with geometric motifs resembling cuneiform signs, "steps and stairs" patterns forming rectangular shapes, and parallel lines. These motifs, arranged in groups over the whole surface, constitute the main decoration of the stelae. But notwithstanding the local tradition it must be observed that the divinity represented on these stelae and on the pottery is not the *suche*, the fish found in the high mountain lakes of this area, but the feline which is found everywhere in Peru.

Tiahuanaco

The Tiahuanaco culture undoubtedly belongs to the Florescent Epoch, and from its very beginnings undoubtedly also shows a link with Huari culture. I believe that it represents a development of the Huari culture on the high plateau.

Standing on an exceptionally inhospitable site at very high altitude, Tiahuanaco is one of the most sacred shrines dedicated to the cult of the feline in the highland areas of Peru. Its red-coloured pottery is notable for its incense-burners in the form of a feline or condor, or sometimes funnel-shaped, and for a series of jars similar to those of Cuzco. There are also globular vessels with necks and with tubes on the sides for drinking from; jars in truncated cone shape with flared sides, and truncated-cone jars with handles; elongated vessels with handles; globular amphoras with handles; pots with two small handles on the sides; bottle-shaped jars; globular vessels, of flattened and elongated shape, with handles; tripod cups; and red jars representing human heads. The motifs are usually geometric – stepped lines, parallel lines, heads of felines or condors. They are painted in strong colours or in black or white, and are usually decorated with white lines. There are also some jars painted a brilliant black, with a slip. The most complicated motifs we find are the figure of a feline carrying an axe and a trophy head and a representation of the feline as an animal with an eye formed by a condor's head.

Tiahuanaco is also notable for its great buildings and for its geometrically patterned monumental sculpture. The statues are usually elongated slabs, in a stylised form which in some of them seems primitive but in others shows great sculptural skill.

The carving of the great gateway of Tiahuanaco is vigorously stylised, with its winged figures carrying sceptres and the multitude of condors' heads which form appendages to their bodies. There are also a number of stelae covered with delicate carvings of figures similar to those on the gateway and also of animal figures. The head of the idol of Conchamarca, too, is covered with the same handsome patterns, which are characteristic of Tiahuanaco sculpture everywhere.

144

Wendell Bennett found in this area sculptures of fairly primitive workmanship but of great beauty, also representing seated idols, like the Pocotic figures in the church at Tiahuanaco, and a number of monoliths which are also of great beauty. The idols in the geometric style, which may be as much as 25 feet high, are also covered with very delicate carving.

The buildings of the Kalasasaya type are of considerable size, and are constructed of large roughly hewn blocks laid in courses, with the spaces filled in by smaller, slightly polished, stones.

The pottery of Tiahuanaco is found all over the high plateau of Peru and in Bolivia. A number of different stages can be distinguished, beginning with Chiripa and ending with a decadent phase; but this is a subject of which space does not permit a full discussion. The important point to note, however, is that – as the work of Peruvian archaeologists has demonstrated – the centre of the culture called Tiahuanaco or Tiahuanacoid is not at Tiahuanaco itself: it is at Huari, in the Department of Ayacucho. It is clear that the pottery of Tiahuanaco is related to the pottery of Huari and that both types must have had a common origin. I will go further and maintain that the pottery of Tiahuanaco is derived from the pottery of Huari, as I noted when discussing the expansion of the Huari civilisation. But in spreading on to the high plateau Huari pottery took on individual characteristics which differentiated it from the style found in its area of origin.

Inca

It is not my intention at this point to discuss the Inca culture, which appeared in the Florescent Epoch and later, in the Imperial Epoch, expanded and conquered the whole of Peru. Large numbers of remains in and around Cuzco bear witness to the different stages of cultural development of this mighty empire.

In architecture we have gigantic monolithic structures like the walls of Sacsahuamán, splendid palaces in multicoloured stone, and buildings like those at Machu Picchu constructed of large stones separated by smaller ones. Finally there are the walls of the last phase built in small convex-faced blocks.

In pottery there is no similar variety. The only type to be mentioned is Quilque, belonging to a stage before the Inca period; and no association has been found between this and any of the buildings.

In accordance with the plan of this work, however, we shall discuss the Inca empire when we come to the Imperial Epoch, the period at which this people achieved its greatest heights.

And so we come to the end of the Florescent Epoch, the classical period of Peruvian civilisation in which the various cultures crystallised, reached their full flowering and – in many cases – began to decline. It was in this period of culmination that the peoples of pre-Columbian Peru reached the peak of their achievement in the arts and sciences, in inventive spirit, in religious belief, in every aspect of their material and spiritual life. Step by step, each people forged its own culture and solved its own particular problems. All these cultures were vigorous and firmly established, for their creative spirit and their faith were vigorous too. They were monotheists, worshipping the anthropomorphic feline who was the religious centre of their life; and on this profound and vigorous faith were built the splendid cultures which have left an immortal record in the panorama of history.

With the Florescent Epoch ends the cultural cycle which led up in successive stages to the classical period of the various cultures which grew up on the basis of elements developed in the Formative Epoch. From north to south of Peru there was an exchange of cultural elements which made it possible for this whole complex of peoples to develop along similar lines. In spite of this interchange, however, these peoples did not unite; and each culture maintained its independence within the framework of a general advance towards greater achievement.

Thus the Florescent Epoch comes to an end at the moment when the various cultures are beginning to decline. In the arts the baroque is dominant, offering a portent of things to come. The peoples of Peru lose their strength and vigour, and the ground is prepared for the developments that are to follow in the Epoch of Fusion.

THE EPOCH OF FUSION

V

Imperial Huari

The people of Huari, confident in their strength and power, now set out to conquer Peru. Their culture had probably been in existence for a thousand years and was now at its peak. Their first raid no doubt took them from the mountains of Ayacucho through the ravines into the Ica, Nazca and Palpa valleys; then they conquered Arequipa and continued northward, bringing under their sway all the peoples of the Andes and the coastal area. And wherever their armies passed the Huaris imposed their arts and their customs. The religious beliefs of the subject peoples presented no obstacle to their advance, for all alike worshipped the same feline god. The remains left by the Huaris, however, show that they were skilled in the art of government and exercised moderation and understanding in imposing their rule.

The Huari invasion explains why we find throughout Peru a stratum of pottery with Huari characteristics – the pottery which has mistakenly been called Tiahuanaco or Tiahuanacoid. In its forms and its decorative techniques this pottery has no connection with the pottery of Tiahuanaco, with the exception of certain features which are due to the relationship which we have already noted to exist between the cultures of Tiahuanaco and Huari. If we are to avoid misconceptions it is essential to get into the habit of calling this pottery Huari, and not by the name of Tiahuanaco which it has borne for so many years – an error which arose from disregarding the real place of origin of a type of pottery found all over Peru.

This pottery persists with its own forms and colours; but sometimes it mingles with the local culture to produced mixed forms like Lambayeque-Huari, Mochica-Huari, or the admixture of Nazca elements which we find in the South Huari culture.

The Huari conquerors showed that they could adapt themselves to their surroundings and adopt the customs prevailing in each area they occupied: for example, the modes of burial in the north are different from those found in the south.

Thus we find an extraneous element introduced into the development of the Peruvian cultural complex as a mountain people leaves its imprint on all the cultures of the Florescent Epoch. This results in the fusion of the new culture with the various existing cultures, and I call the period during which this occurs the Epoch of Fusion. It could be given other names, but whatever the name the basic situation is still the same: the culture of the conquerors is fused with the cultures of the conquered and imposes on them many of its own peculiar characteristics.

I divide the pottery found along the coast into North Huari A, Central Huari A and South Huari A. It is unnecessary to give a detailed description of each of these types, which show only slight differences. We find the original forms of Huari pottery persisting, with a predominance of jars with double spout and bridge and double vessels consisting of a jar and a figure. The jars tend to be of rather elongated shape. The globular vessels have handles on the sides; and there are also bottle-shaped jars.

North Huari A

The pottery of the north is extremely fine. Examples of this are provided by the pottery found in the Department of Ica; and we have a number of jars from Chiclayo and Piura which are of equal quality, as a result of the influence of the Lambayeque culture. The Huari motifs were preserved with greater purity in the north than in the south; but in the central area the Huari pottery has neither the brilliant colouring nor the fine modelling found in the north and south.

In the south the tombs take the form of large trenches containing the mummy bundles. The bodies are in a sitting position, with their knees bent close up against their chests, so that they look like limbless torsos with neither arms nor legs. They were swathed in cotton shrouds and then wrapped in thick material which gave the bundles the outline of a human figure. As a rule food was placed at the level of the head. Finally the mummies were enclosed in splendid fabrics and surrounded by pottery vessels. These fabrics are very highly prized by collectors for their colouring and their abstract patterns: so beautiful are they, indeed, that we regard our collection in the Rafael Larco Herrera Museum as the second finest collection of textiles in the world. The mummies wore wigs made up of hundreds of slender tresses interwoven in attractive geometric patterns and tied by threads.

In the central coastal area and in the north the dead were buried in a flexed position in irregularly shaped pits. In the Santa valley we found one very fine house-shaped tomb with its walls decorated in a pattern of lozenges, and with

102

103

104

106

107

111

112

114

115

116→

118

rectangular niches built into the sides. The sarcophagus contained the finest and most delicate pieces of Huari pottery ever found in northern Peru, along with gold articles, necklaces and masks of exceptional quality.

The pottery of the central area has neither the brilliance nor the perfection of modelling of the specimens found in the north; and its colours seem pale in comparison with those found in the pottery of the north and south.

Huari-Lambayeque

As we have already noted, the Huari culture mingled with the cultures of the Lambayeque area to produce the Huari-Lambayeque style. The predominant forms are spout-and-bridge jars with a base, amphoras with a neck and lateral handles, and stirrup-spouted jars; for we must not forget that we are concerned here with a mixed culture including northern elements. The commonest colours are black, red and cream. The characteristic Huari motif of a circle and black spot is still used, and we also find the Greek key patterns and the volutes typical of the highland culture, as well as the Lambayeque deity on bottle-shaped jars. *(Plate 74)*

In the Chicama valley our excavations yielded double jars with a representation on the front part of a warrior or other figure with characteristic Mochica features. The finest specimens are a combination of the polychrome painting and the double spout and bridge characteristic of the Huari culture with the motifs painted in several colours of the Mochicas. There are also globular vessels with double spout and bridge, coloured cream and ochre and with Mochica motifs.

Humaya

In the central area the Huari culture is associated with the culture of Lima, producing the pottery of Humaya which uses the orange colouring inherited from Lima along with shapes and painted decorative themes from the Huari culture. In the south the main types are head-jars with double spout and bridge, globular vessels of truncated cone shape with double spout and bridge, jars with stylised heads of Huari type, and globular vessels with a neck on which is modelled a human head. The colours used on pottery of this period, both on the coast and in the highland areas, are light beige, dark beige, orange, white, black, ochre and a greyish-cream colour.

Rukana

In the south Huari mingled with Chanca, just as it had earlier with Nazca, to produce the Rukana culture. In my view this belongs to the Florescent Epoch rather than to the Epoch of Fusion: it is related to the Huari culture rather than a derivative of it. One of the decorative motifs is the chevron, which is found on almost all the globular vessels of Rukana and clearly indicates a connection with the Huari culture.

The pottery is coloured bright red. There are double jars of anthropomorphic type with spout and bridge, jars in the shape of birds, and others representing crabs; we have one bird-shaped jar with a stirrup spout. But most of the pottery consists of spherical vessels with a small neck and simple pots. The decorative themes are symbolical and highly idealised, and are surrounded by the white circle with a black spot characteristic of the Huari culture. We also find representations of the feline in stylised form, and a variety of motifs – S-shaped figures, crosses, snakes, short straight lines and starfishes – painted in whitish-grey or black and cream. *(Plate 86)*

The finest pottery of this culture is that found at Ocoña, near the archaeological site of La Victoria, by the expedition which worked here in 1943 with the most exact scientific method. The vessels are of considerable size and designed for ornament, and are in the shape of large amphoras. The neck is formed by a modelled human head showing the highest artistic skill. These vases demonstrate the close relationship between the pottery of Rukana and of Huari; for their geometric patterns and figures of felines show a most striking similarity to the decorative themes of Huari.

According to Tello the textiles found with the Rukana pottery are of very high quality, and the tombs are large chambers built of stone and clay. The body is wrapped in rough country-made cloths and wears a cloak of the same material.

It may be that this pottery is the origin of the beige-coloured and smoked jars. The former type is covered with a beige slip and is decorated in black, white, red and orange. The smoked jars are usually decorated with stylised patterns and are painted in black, beige and ochre. There is only a limited number of types – they can be counted on the fingers of one hand – but they have characteristics which differentiate them from other types.

In these four styles, including Huari, the decoration is surrounded by black lines, except on rare occasions when white paint has been used.

North Huari B

The Huari culture must have maintained itself in the conquered territory for a considerable period; and this is no doubt why we find it, in northern, central and southern Peru, entering a phase of decadence which I call Huari B. In the north this decadence is shown by a preference for very variegated colour schemes and a tendency to give up the use of the Huari colours. The same pottery types are found, along with some new ones. This pottery is easily recognised not only by its extensive use of white circles with black spots but because the whole surface of the jars is covered with ornament which reveals at once the source from which it is derived and the decadent style in which it is expressed. The representations of felines, of human faces and of all the other indigenous Huari themes become grotesque, and the main subjects are surrounded by an elaborate geometric pattern. There are some jars from which the colour has disappeared altogether: on top of the white slip the only decoration consists of black lines, like the lines round the polychrome decoration of Huari pottery. *(Plate 107)*

In this period there was still a cult of the feline, who is represented with a girdle of two-headed snakes and wearing ear ornaments in the form of snakes.

This pottery, which I call North Huari B, is found not only all along the coast of northern Peru and in the interior but also occurs in abundance in the area of Huarmey, Casma and Nepeña, as well as at Chimbote. On the basis of this distribution Dr. Tello gave the name of Huaylas to this pottery. It persisted longer in this area than in the north because the Chimú kingdom which arose in the Santa Catalina valley set out on a movement of expansion and conquest which took it as far as Tumbes and perhaps even into Ecuador. In this territory, there-fore, we find Chimú pottery, and this later extended its domain southward as far as Paramonga. It is reasonable to suppose that this conquest favoured Huari culture, which continued to develop in this area, while the rest of the northern coast of Peru was incorporated in the Chimú empire; and in consequence we find an abundance of this pottery in the area.

North Huari C

In the area between Chao and Huarmey we find what I call North Huari C, a period of total decadence in the Huari pottery of this area. It is black and poorly fired, and colour has completely disappeared. The art of pottery has fallen into neglect: neither the materials nor the colours were properly selected, as is shown by the greyish-black colouring of the pottery. The decoration, in a faint reflection of the Huari style, is still in relief. The potters no longer took the trouble to burnish their work, and the surface is therefore dull.

The bodies were still buried in a flexed position, for the Huaris completely changed the form of burial. They also introduced the practice of direct tabular skull deformation.

Central Huari B

The decadent stage of Huari is also found in the central area, and here I have given it the name of Central Huari B. The use of painting disappears completely, and the pottery – coarse, porous, poorly polished and even more poorly made – retains the natural colour of the terracotta. The decoration is painted in red on areas of cream, or occasionally in white on areas of red. The patterns, mostly geometric, are poorly drawn. The shapes are clumsy but we can still recognise the characteristic Huari forms. The potters of this phase also used reliefs to decorate their jars, and we sometimes find them adopting certain local forms. *(Plate 30)*

Teatino

At Teatino we find a red-coloured pottery, well polished and with incised decoration which shows some sign of Huari derivation. Clearly this pottery is related to Huari, but it is difficult to be certain about the exact relationship, for the incised ornament does not enable us to make comparisons. In general the decoration is made up of very simple geometric elements.

South Huari A

We must now consider the situation in the south. Here too Huari enters a decadent phase. The jars lose the brilliant colouring which characterised Huari A, and their surface is unpolished; and in the decoration there is a noticeable loss of purity of line. There is only a limited range of types, the commonest being globular vessels with representations of human faces on the neck. *(Plates 87, 88)*

We find the same kind of thing in the Chanca B culture. The characteristic Chanca designs disappear and are replaced by decoration typical of the Santa culture. The pottery loses its refinement, and no longer has the polish and the finish of Chanca work of the Florescent Epoch.

Huari of Arequipa

Pottery of Huari type has also been found at Chuquibamba in the Arequipa area, with a fairly wide geographical distribution. It is red in colour, with forms similar to those of Huari, but decorated in black. Here too the pottery of Huari is in decadence.

The Epoch of Fusion, which I am sometimes tempted to call an epoch of confusion, has thus reached its final term. There has been a general degeneration of culture, involving both the areas in which the various cultures arose and the areas to which they extended. But all the peoples who had in the past achieved greatness were still inspired by the hope of building anew and the urge towards fresh achievements. Now they were to come together, taking the best from the cultures of the past to create new cultures different from those of the Florescent Epoch and the Epoch of Fusion. And, looking at their later work, we can see that their faith, their virile resolution and their clear-sighted intelligence were sufficient to enable them to achieve their aim and organise new peoples with new political ideas and, perhaps, fresh religious conceptions.

THE IMPERIAL EPOCH

VI

The peoples who were thus brought together needed powerful and intelligent leaders who could guide them safely and confidently on the path they had chosen to follow. They had to restore their strength – materially, spiritually and politically – after the period of confusion if they were to attain the greatness and power which they sought. Moved by this ambition, there grew up in the north of Peru the great Chimú kingdom, which succeeded in gaining control of the northern coastal area from Tumbes to Paramonga, and indeed seems to have extended into Ecuador, to judge from the remains which have been found there. In the central area there was Chancay and, in the Ica valley, the kingdom of the Chinchas, which extended from Chincha to Palpa. At Arequipa there were the Pukinas, at Cuzco the Quechuas. Elsewhere in the country there were other groups of lesser importance.

The art of this period lacks the quality of the cultures of the Florescent Epoch. It is an age of material progress, but it has lost the power to create beautiful things which the peoples of the Formative Epoch possessed. The men of this period were warriors, conquerors and great builders; but, with some exceptions, their work was not of high artistic value. They showed great skill in certain techniques and trades, but always with a utilitarian object in view: they were not concerned, as their predecessors had been, to combine the beautiful and the useful. Instead they were moved by purely materialistic considerations, producing goods in quantity to meet the needs of a rapidly expanding population. In the course of time the natural growth of the population had greatly increased the number of mouths to feed, and the necessary food supply could no longer be found in the valleys, where every available piece of ground had been irrigated and brought into cultivation, and in the desert areas which had been reclaimed for agriculture. It was necessary, therefore, to supplement the inadequate resources of the land by seeking additional food supplies from the sea.

The older towns had been built in the valleys, fairly evenly spaced over the area of settlement and sited with strategic considerations in mind. Now they were built near the sea, preferably near harbours where the small boats of the fishermen could find shelter. Examples of this are Chiquitoy Viejo, Pacatnamú (Pacasmayo), Chanchan in the Santa Catalina valley, the great Chincha cities and the many ruined sites in the Chancay and other valleys – all situated near the sea.

The towns of this period were no longer merely clusters of houses huddled round a temple or fortress: they were properly planned, regularly laid out and well built. This is true at any rate of the newly established towns: no doubt, however, the existing towns continued to be occupied.

Then, just when the new kingdoms were reaching their greatest splendour in the middle period of the Imperial Epoch, a new conquering power threatened the southern Andes and set out to occupy the whole of Peru, establishing what might be called the Second Empire. This new empire was to swallow up all the existing kingdoms, to extend into northern Chile and Argentina, and to absorb Bolivia and the territory now known as Ecuador. All these peoples were now brought into a single empire – though in some areas, for example in the north, this was of short duration. And wherever they went the conquerors imposed their art and their religious ideas, altering the patterns of local culture, transforming existing arts and institutions and beliefs.

Chimú

I propose to begin by discussing the kingdom of Chimú, disregarding for this purpose the information provided by the chroniclers and the legends in which some people still believe.

The Chimús were a powerful people whose kingdom, as I have already noted, extended from Ecuador to Paramonga. Warriors of tireless fighting spirit and unflinching courage, they confronted the imperial Inca armies at Paramonga, and would have beaten them but for the arrival of thirty thousand Inca reinforcements from Cuzco. Fearing defeat, the Chimús set fire to their capital city of Chanchan, in whose artistic and architectural beauty they took special pride. They finally agreed to submit only when an alliance was concluded between the Inca and the Great Chimú; and it is said that the Great Chimú was borne through Cajamarca side by side with the Inca in a litter with a golden throne.

The Chimús were skilled in the art of governing, and great builders. Chanchan, a town of sun-dried brick, is one of the finest cities of ancient Peru. It was divided into a number of independent rectangular compounds, each of which had reservoirs containing enough water to meet the needs of its population. Some of these great rectangles were enclosed in almost impregnable *pisé* walls more than 20 feet high, standing within a few yards of each other. They contain the remains

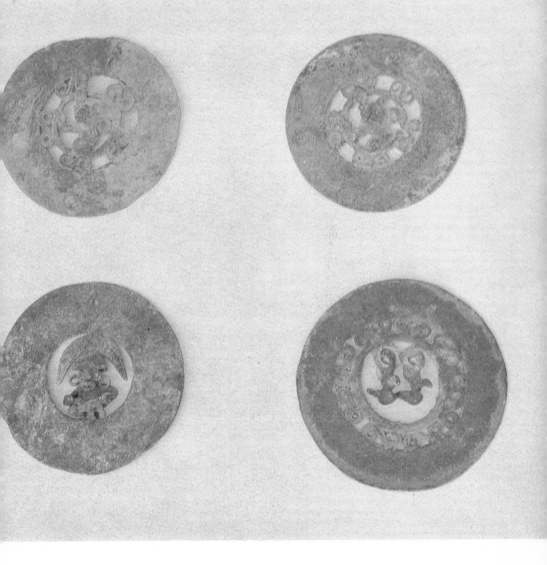

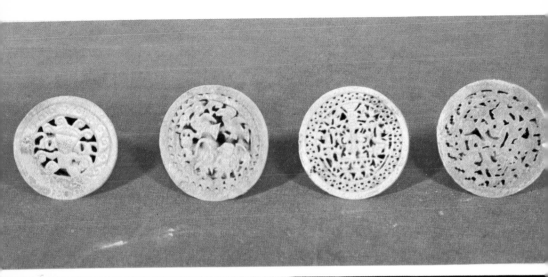

125

129

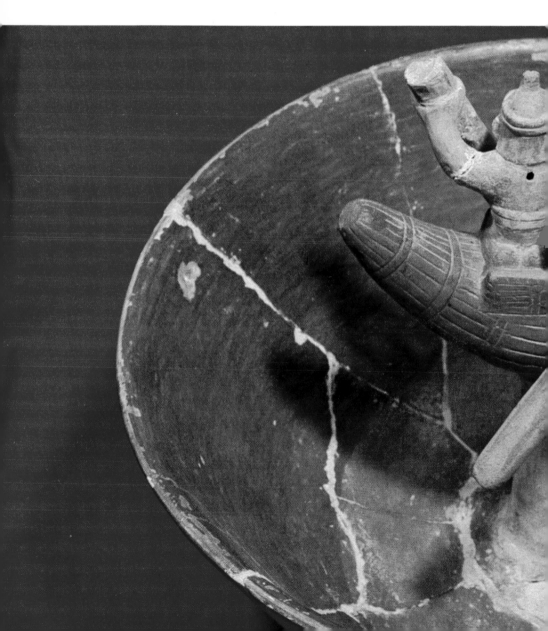

133

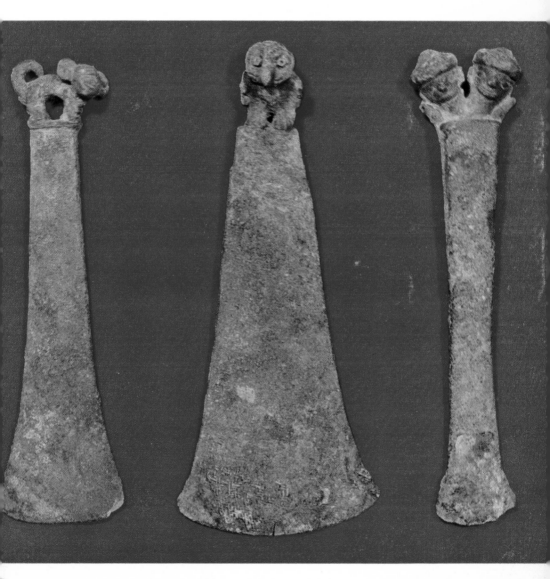

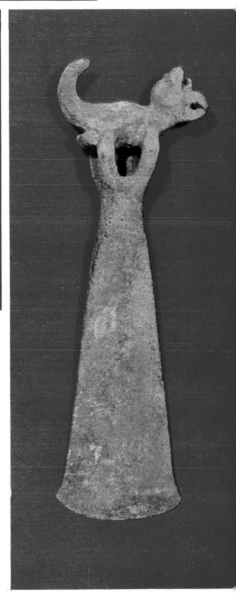

of buildings which seem to have been palaces standing several stories high, built on a plan not very different from that which our best modern architects, using the methods and equipment of the present day, might have drawn. The walls were splendidly decorated with arabesques and a variety of patterns – anthropomorphic, zoomorphic and geometric – covering their whole surface.

Unfortunately the ravages of fire and the passage of time have largely destroyed this decoration. Part of it has been restored; but I must record with great regret that the restoration is quite unsatisfactory, having been done by people without the experience required for a task of such complexity and delicacy, and without regard to proper archaeological criteria.

The Chimús used large adobe bricks for the foundations of their buildings, and medium-sized adobes, like those used by the Mochicas, for the walls. For the roofs and door lintels they used a mortar containing a high proportion of gravel and stone. The rooms in their buildings were small, but looked out on to large interior courtyards with ramps. The terracotta reliefs, which were executed in large sections and not – as with the Mochicas – on rectangular bricks laid to form the wall, were sometimes painted white or cream. The reservoirs within each district were shaped like inverted pyramids, and were faced with stone.

It is interesting to note that the Chimús had abandoned the type of pyramidal construction used in earlier periods. Unfortunately space does not permit a full discussion of the architecture and layout of Chanchan or of the various types of Chimú building: we must be content to recall that Chanchan was one of the largest cities of ancient Peru, stretching from the present-day town of Trujillo to the neighbourhood of Huanchaco.

The Chimú pottery points clearly to the origin of this culture, for it shows a mingling of elements from the Mochica, Huari and Lambayeque cultures. First Lambayeque, coming from the north, contributed its share. Since the time of Max Uhle much energy has been devoted to the quest for a "middle Chimú" style which would have provided a link between Mochica and Chimú; but no such style could be found, for the Mochica and Chimú styles were not linked by any single culture but by a number of cultures which combined different elements to create this new civilisation of the Imperial Epoch. Almost overnight, the pottery became black: only occasionally do we find a jar which is brick red in colour. This black colouring is clearly derived from Lambayeque, as is the monkey which appears at the junction between the handle and the spout. The pouble spout and bridge, and the base found on most of the jars, also come from Lambayeque and Huari. Another element from Lambayeque is the feline deity with almond-shaped eyes which is found on the Chimú pottery, though with simpler and less elaborate decoration than in Lambayeque. The pottery is not notable for the high quality of its modelling. The designs are repeated many times over, for this was mass production in which the output was counted in thousands: as we have noted, the potters had to meet the demands of an increasing population and to supply the material required for the cult of the dead.

The decorative motifs of this pottery and the range of types are still the same. There are globular vessels; stirrup-spouted jars with figures; spout -and-bridge jars with a base in the form of a truncated cone; double jars with double spouts and bridge; globular amphoras; and bottle-shaped jars with a handle. These vessels are covered with brilliant black; a few are decorated with motifs in relief – anthropomorphic, zoomorphic or phytomorphic. To differentiate the planes the potters used unpolished surfaces covered with small knobs. Modelling had become of secondary importance, though the anthropomorphic and zoomorphic figures were still under the influence of Lambayeque modelling techniques. *(Plates 66, 77)*

The Chimús inherited their goldsmithing knowledge and techniques from the people of Lambayeque and the Mochicas. The gold jewellery of Chimú is often confused with that of Lambayeque, of which typical examples are the finds made at Batán Grande, although their goldsmith's work, like their pottery, is quite different. There have been no finds at Chanchan of the large *tumis* (semicircular knives) or the repoussé metal vases of varying shapes and with varying decoration which have been discovered at Lambayeque. The works of the Chimú goldsmiths are of extreme delicacy and excellent finish, and they also surpass Lambayeque work in the high quality of their decorative techniques – repoussé, openwork and engraving. The decorative themes are equally different – the main theme at L ambayeque being the feline deity, whereas Chimú art has a whole range of subjects. The ear ornaments of Chanchan are in repoussé work of unrivalled delicacy, and its engraved gold and silver vases are masterpieces of filigree work. We have in the Rafael Larco Herrera Museum a complete set of gold ornaments – a breastplate with repoussé decoration ending with thin sheets of gold in the form of feathers, ear ornaments, necklaces, shoulder-pieces, and a crown with four gold plumes ornamented in repoussé. One can imagine the majestic appearanc of the high dignitaries arrayed in brightly coloured garments and adorned wit a profusion of gold ornaments such as these. *(Plates 120, 121, 126)*

The Chimús used large ceremonial vessels, cups which were probably intended for offering blood to their god on the occasion of human sacrifices.

They were also skilled silversmiths, and knew the technique of producing the alloys they required. Their ear ornaments, their dishes with double bottoms and their gourd-shaped vessels are the finest examples of ancient Peruvian work known. Their methods of casting, engraving and doing repoussé work have never been surpassed. They used copper with outstanding skill. The objects they produced by the *cire perdue* process are of the highest quality and can stand comparison with the finest production of any period or any country in the world. They also used platinum, casting from it statuettes and representations of ceremonial scenes. *(Plates 94, 102, 122)*

The Chimús were also past masters in the art of textile working, as is shown by the clothes found at Chanchan, perfectly preserved as if they had just been laid away in the niches in which they were discovered. These particular articles seem to have been warriors' garments made of plain thick white material – a short shirt, a skirt or kilt, a loincloth and a long cloak with two strips of material which fastened on the breast. We possess also some fine pieces of cloth magnificently patterned in brilliant colours. The Chimús had a liking for large patterns, with a preference for anthropomorphic or sometimes zoomorphic themes.

The people of Chimú wore splendid ear pendants in repoussé and openwork, head-bands, and brooches fastening the knot with which they tied their cloaks. In addition their garments might be adorned with a whole array of small silver ornaments representing fish, little bells, spangles of different sizes, and a great variety of other articles. They also wore nose ornaments, bracelets or necklaces of turquoise, lapis lazuli or quartz. In the tomb containing a child's body was found a silver gilt box in which were a little girl's toys – a small bed, a carpet, a basin for washing clothes, a collection of kitchen utensils, mirrors and weaving implements. Everything was in miniature, faithfully reproducing the full-size articles used in everyday life.

The Chimús were fond of luxury, as is shown by some of the objects found at Chanchan such as the large double-bottomed silver gilt dishes which were apparently intended for use at banquets. Some of these dishes are as much as 2½ feet across. The object of the double bottom was to prevent the guests from burning their fingers. There are also some fine silver dishes decorated with zoomorphic designs in repoussé, and silver vessels inlaid with turquoise, mother-of-pearl and *spondylus*, producing the effect of a mosaic. *(Plate 92)*.

We have seen how the pottery of Chimú is often confused with that of Lambayeque, and a similar mistake is sometimes made with the goldsmithing work. When Chimú work is compared with Lambayeque the latter is seen at once to be clumsy and of poor quality. The engraving, the repoussé work and the casting of Chimú were never equalled by the people of Lambayeque. The only respect in which the advantage lies with Lambayeque is the quantity of gold used; for the Chimús never had adequate supplies of the metal. Nevertheless I have seen in a private collection a magnificent display of gold jewellery and other objects of the most delicate workmanship, weighing altogether something like sixty pounds. Some of these are now in the Museum of Anthropology, where they are among the finest pieces on show.

The Chimús were also excellent sculptors, as is shown by a number of magnificent idols in carob wood, some of them covered with silver and with a gold mask. We also have in the Rafael Larco Herrera Museum a vase covered with an inlay of mother-of-pearl and bone representing a feline which forms part of a ceremonial *maté* dish. *(Plate 98)*

The Chimús buried their dead in a sitting position in irregularly shaped pits, and practised direct tabular skull deformation. At Chanchan burial enclosures have been found in which the mummies were arranged round the walls, surrounded by all the funerary offerings, with a frieze of anthropomorphic and zoomorphic figures in mother-of-pearl and *spondylus*. One of these friezes was covered with condors with widespread wings and with a pearl hanging by a gold thread from a hole in their beak.

Warriors, conquerors, builders and master weavers as they were, the Chimús nevertheless had certain features which demonstrated the spiritual depths within them: the flame kindled by their ancestors in forging their art and their culture was not yet extinguished.

Chancay

The kingdom of Chancay extended from Huacho to Lima and Lurín, where some jars belonging to this culture have been found.

The transition from Central Huari B to Chancay is easy to follow. The pottery of Chancay has the same dull surface as that of the earlier culture, and we also find in it some of the forms known in Central Huari B. My own observations and studies suggest that there are three stages of Chancay: a type of red pottery with white and black decoration, similar to the pottery of Huari; cream jars with brown decoration; and white pottery, without any colour, which shows that the potters were concerned purely with form rather than decoration. This pottery shows both Huari and Chimú influences. Various types have been found – double jars, figure jars, spout-and-bridge jars. The commonest shapes are globular amphoras with a handle, poorly modelled zoomorphic figures, elongated jars and globular vessels with a base. There are also gourd-shaped vessels, ranging from shallow dishes to bowls with rounded sides, large elongated globular vessels with handles, and jars of anthropomorphic form. There are great numbers of large figures of naked men or women, which are not containers but funerary offerings. The decoration is often geometric and covers the whole surface of the jars; the usual colours are cream and black or brown on cream. Space does not permit a complete listing of the geometric patterns employed, ranging from parallel lines close together to the most complicated combinations of geometric elements. *(Plates 64, 76, 78, 113, 119)*

We also find anthropomorphic and zoomorphic decoration – stylised versions of snakes and fish, small animals, or human figures in relief.

But this great culture is notable above all for its textiles; for the weavers of Chancay were magnificently skilled in all the techniques of their craft and in the use of a great range of colours. Some of their work can stand comparison with the finest achievements of other cultures. But their main claim to distinction is their technical mastery, which enabled them to produce the most marvellous embroideries and lace, and to combine their brilliant colours into a harmonious pattern. The designs are mostly based on stylised anthropomorphic, zoomorphic and geometric motifs. Compared with the textiles the pottery of Chancay is of secondary importance. *(Plates 140, 141, 146)*

The population must by this time have been very large. In the Lauri cemetery, in spite of the continuing vandalism, pottery of Chancay type and fine textiles are continually being found. It was the practice in this culture to bury the dead with all the things they had used in life, particularly weaving implements. The tombs are irregularly shaped pits, sometimes covered with adobe and containing large mummy bundles like those of Huari, or rectangular chambers with *pisé* walls or merely excavated in the ground. The mummy is wrapped up in a rectangular bundle with the offerings of textiles. In some of the tombs the mummy is lying in a hammock above a rectangular cavity roofed with logs or reeds.

Along with the cloths we find looms, spindles, baskets containing all the implements used in weaving and spinning, reeds on which the coloured threads used in the splendid geometric patterns of Chancay are spooled, balls of thread, and reed crosses on which threads of different colours are wound to produce a pattern of concentric lozenges like the so-called "God's eyes" of the Huichole Indians of Mexico. There are also rush baskets, charming groups of dolls representing a variety of scenes, small trees made from twisted thread, complete with leaves and birds, rounded fragments of iron, and objects in wood. Dogs and guinea-pigs were sometimes buried along with the dead man.

Chincha

The kingdom of Chincha lay farther to the south: fragments of its pottery have been found at Lurín and Chancay, and its territory extended as far as Palpa.

Here too art entered a decadent phase. We have only isolated fragments of particular forms and decorative themes, unexpectedly occurring along with examples of the ornamental styles characteristic of this pottery. Art undergoes a complete change, becoming geometric and stylised – perhaps under the influence of textile patterns, which were of course conditioned by the warp and the woof. Anthropomorphic, zoomorphic and geometric themes are combined into harmonious patterns. Some jars look as if they were surrounded by a woven girdle of ornament. The influence of the Rukana style can also be seen. The jars are coloured red or, more usually, cream; the decoration is in red, cream, grey or black.

It is interesting to note that the line and the shape of the lips are derived from Huari. There are pots with thick rims, globular vessels with a neck and a handle, flat dishes with scenes painted on the inside surface, vessels with flaring curved sides, anthropomorphic and a few zoomorphic figures.

Considerable quantities of bone implements have been found, in particular the upper part of small scales, and also flutes.

190

Mortar was used in the construction of buildings – in particular the temples and fortresses which were built on low hillocks.

The Chincha textiles are magnificent, maintaining the standards set by the great weavers of this area. The main decorative themes of the textiles, as of the pottery, are vigorously stylised geometric patterns. In delicacy of technique the Chincha fabrics hold what must be a world record: we possess examples with 398 threads to the inch, a figure which had never previously been achieved and has never been equalled since. This material demonstrates not only the incredible dexterity of the weavers but also the manual skill of the women who could spin the slender threads used in this marvellous fabric.

Pukina

The Pukina culture developed during the same period round Arequipa, which was its main centre. Its pottery is derived not so much from Huari as from Tiahuanaco on the high plateau, whose pottery style extended by way of Puno into Bolivia and had a considerable influence on the north of Chile.

The forms found here are mostly of truncated cone shape. There are elongated jars with a lip, globular vessels including some with a neck and a handle, wide-mouthed jars, and vessels with a handle and a spout on the side. The pottery is coloured red, with white motifs and patterns in black with a white spot and black areas between white lines. Geometric designs predominate, including some reminiscent of those found in Tiahuanaco pottery.

Burials are found either in pits or in chambers of undressed stone, poorly built and with no artistic merit, in a style which could be described as decadent Tiahuanaco. At Chuquibamba in the Department of Arequipa we find pottery with much more noticeable Huari characteristics; and tombs have also been found containing pottery of great refinement belonging to this culture.

This concludes our discussion of this period of the Imperial Epoch.

Imperial Inca

While the great kingdoms were taking shape another highland culture from the Collao area was gradually coming into existence. Then in course of time it suddenly developed a new energy which carried it forward to greater things. This was the empire founded by Manco Capac – to whom legend ascribed the special lustre of descending from the sun – and ruled by him and his successors the Incas. This warlike people, rigidly organised under leaders of high intelligence and political capacity, were not content to dominate the territory of Collao, but established the great empire of Tahuantisuyo with its capital at Cuzco.

I agree with Montesinos, however, in thinking that the Inca empire did not begin with Manco Capac and Mama Ocllo: I believe that there was another empire before this. This is demonstrated by the aryballi – those typical forms of Inca pottery – which are found already developed and with Huari decorative themes, showing that this culture was at its peak when the Huari hordes overran the whole of Peru. It is easy to believe that this empire lasted not merely for a few years but for centuries; and it is reasonable to suppose that there must have been a number of cultures succeeding one another in the area occupied by the Quechas before the 11th century. I do not propose to study the legendary material or to concern myself with the manner in which the Ayar brothers founded this empire. What is certain is that we find in Quechua territory the pottery of Chanapata with characteristic incised designs belonging to the end of the Formative Epoch: and that there were, therefore, cultures in the Cuzco area which developed gradually until they attained their highest expression. The pottery of Quilque shows us an Inca pottery style in the process of formation.

As noted above, the empire of Manco Capac and Mama Ocllo was formed in the 11th century. It was ruled by a succession of thirteen Incas, eight of whom controlled only an area round Cuzco. These were:

1. Manco Capac
2. Sinchi Roca
3. Lloque Yupanqui
4. Mayta Capac
5. Capac Yupanqui
6. Inca Roca
7. Yahuar Huacac
8. Viracocha
9. Pachacutec Inca Yupanqui
10. Tupac Inca Yupanqui
11. Huayna Capac
12. Huascar
13. Atahuallpa

According to Rowe, the great conquests began with Pachacutec, who ruled from 1438 to 1471, and Tupac Yupanqui (1471–1493). Then came Huayna Capac, who ruled from 1493 to 1525. The reign of Huascar was cut short by his quarrel with his brother Atahuallpa. Huayna Capac had conquered Ecuador; and Atahuallpa, who ruled from 1522 to 1533, was the son of awo man from Quito.

Atahuallpa defeated Huascar and sent an army of forty thousand men to Cuzco to seize the empire. This campaign began with the conquest of the Chancas of Abancay and then moved more slowly northward to conquer the territory of Ecuador as far as its boundary with Colombia, and southward to occupy the north of Argentina as far as the River Maule in Chile.

As I have said, I do not propose to use the historical sources as the basis of my discussion of the empire of the Incas. I approach the subject from a purely archaeological point of view, and it is as a specialist in this discipline that I shall seek to consider the Inca period. It is necessary, however, to refer briefly to some essential features in the organisation of the empire.

The Inca empire was based on a legendary institution, the *ayllu* or family kin-group. Some of these claimed to be descended from an animal, a totem, or some sacred place dating back to a very remote period. The Incas used the *ayllus* for their own purposes, turning them into a formal political institution. In place of the former system in which the members of a family could find their own level in society according to their merits, the Incas imposed a political and social system in which the *ayllu* was the smallest unit. With the help of this system the Inca and the political leaders of the empire controlled the *ayllu*, directly or indirectly, and even directed the personal acts of each individual.

The country was divided into four large regions. The State owned all the land, the mines and the livestock, controlled all production, and ensured that all necessary supplies were available to the community. Everyone was required to work according to his productive capacity, and the whole nation thus became an army of organized workers. Personal liberty did not exist. There was a system of public assistance for those in need, but any failure in the performance of the day's allotted task was severely punished. In discussions of this system there has been much talk of agrarian collectivism or of an energetic paternalism; but in fact it can best be described as a socialist state organised in accordance with the conditions of the time and the beliefs, customs and character of the people – and it must be agreed that the Incas and the ruling caste thoroughly understood the people they were dealing with.

The whole territory of the Empire was efficiently governed by a hierarchy of chiefs and under-chiefs, and each of these was visited once a year by an Imperial inspector who was responsible for collecting the statistics necessary for the running of the Empire. The priests also exercised considerable influence over the people.

There was a number of special groups within the population: the *yanaconas* (those exempted from compulsory agricultural labour), the *mamacunas* (the "Virgins of the Sun"), the *acllacunas* (the "chosen women" who were selected for sacrifice on great occasions), and the *hauasipascunas* (the "discarded women" who were not selected for such positions of special honour).

The coronation of the Emperor was a lengthy and a splendid ceremony, involving solemn rituals intended to demonstrate not only his physical capacity but his intellectual and spiritual qualities; and when he died he was surrounded by his favourite wives and his most faithful servants, who were buried with him so that they might minister to his needs in the after-life.

The Incas and their people were, as I have indicated, great warriors as well as skilled organisers. Their weapons were spear-throwers, *bolas* of stone, bronze, iron or silver, bows and arrows, slings, clubs, semicircular knives and axes – the axe being their favourite weapon. Their maces were not merely blunt instruments but were fitted with spikes to cause a piercing wound. For defence they relied on a shield. Their armies were highly organised when in camp, and when in the field were directed in accordance with a system of strategy and tactics which included attacks on the enemy's supplies. This was demonstrated when the Inca army, in order to compel the peoples of the coastal area to submit, cut off their water supply.

The art of the Incas mingled harmoniously with the local styles of the conquered peoples; the fresh current of artistic inspiration brought by these incomers from the highlands adapted itself to local conditions and became predominant. In the north it combined with the Chimú of Lambayeque, Trujillo and other areas to produce the style which I call Chimú-Inca. The proportion of stirrup-spouted jars falls. The monkey which is so characteristic of Chimú is replaced by a "steps and stairs" pattern, a circle or a bird. Colour comes into its own again, but it is Inca colour. The decorative themes, both in painting and in modelling, are geometric. New forms derived from the aryballus begin to appear, like the double aryballus with bridge.

We find in the north new pottery forms which have already been observed at Cuzco – *pacchas* (vessels with long handles) of polychrome terracotta in the form of maces, and models in pottery of the Inca plough, the *taquitaclla*, which reproduce in exact detail the different parts of the implement and show how they fit together. The *pacchas*, exploiting all the modelling skill of the northern peoples, offer a variety of form and colour which are a long way from the art of Cuzco.

From a single tomb in the Chicama valley we took a *paccha* in the form of a portrait head and five maces with the representation of a shield and its attachments. We also found *pacchas* in the form of a snail, which are among the largest found in the area and have the longest handles; beakers *(keros)* with lids; and an aryballus with a smaller vessel of the same kind on the upper part of the side. All this pottery is painted in polychrome, with decorative themes clearly derived from Cuzco, but showing a modelling and painting technique which is not found in the Inca capital.

The Inca rulers took care to bring goldsmiths from the north and establish them in Cuzco so that they might teach the art of which they were past masters. And so this recognition of the high quality of the gold and silver articles produced in a distant province contributed to the development of the goldsmith's art in the wider Andean area.

At this point we may recall the inventories which were prepared listing Atahuallpa's ransom and the treasures sent to Spain by Pizarro as the fifth share of the gold and silver which was due to the Emperor Charles V. These inventories list some pieces of extraordinary size – vessels weighing over sixty pounds, gold animals weighing fifty-nine pounds, gold statues of female figures weighing from thirty-seven to fifty-seven pounds. Nothing comparable to these items has been found at Cuzco: all we have is a few vessels of no artistic interest, some jars scarcely bigger than a thimble, and some small idols – figurines of men and women, cast in a single piece, but of no significance even as examples of goldworking technique. In the northern area we found in an Inca tomb a small headband in gold with spangles, along with funerary offerings of aryballi; the spangles and the method of fixing them showed the influence of northern goldsmithing techniques. There is no doubt that a large part of Atahuallpa's ransom and of the gold which was later sent to Spain belonged to the peoples conquered by the Incas, and that these peoples in turn had inherited this wealth from their predecessors. *(Plate 143)*

The silver objects which have been found are not of any importance either. They include a few small idols, some representations of alpacas and llamas, large fibulas with a small central hole, simple jars with thin flared sides, other jars decorated with a face or two faces, a few globular vessels – and that is all.

The copper objects found include lance points, maces, pins, fibulas, knives, very heavy axes made of an alloy which hardens the metal, and a few objects from Champi containing traces of gold – *tumis* (semicircular knives), some small pieces which served as spear-throwers, and various trinkets and pendants. There are also *tumis* in bronze inlaid with silver, copper and silver knives, baton handles in the form of a jaguar's head, and maces with human figures or many-headed jaguars.

The chroniclers describe the Inca system of communications based on a corps of *chasquis* (messengers or runners); but this was nothing new, for the Indians of the north had used the same system a thousand years before the Inca armies conquered the territory of the Mochicas.

Nor was there anything very new about the great litters in which the Incas and the highest nobles were carried by teams of their vassals. There were also smaller litters for a single person, consisting of a hammock slung from a pole carried on the shoulders of two servants.

Montesinos tells us that the Incas sought to wipe out every reminder of the history of the conquered peoples, or of their traditions, their legends, their religion or any expression of their spiritual life. Accordingly they imposed the death penalty on anyone who used the system of writing current before the Inca conquest. In its place they introduced the *quipu*, a mnemonic device consisting of a series of strings of different colours with knots of different sizes, which could be deciphered only by members of a special caste, the *quipucamayoc*, who thus became the Inca's trusted servants and confidential advisers.

The Incas used the system of main roads for their communications and the movement of their armies; and similarly they exploited the irrigation system they found in their new territories, adapting the experience of other peoples for the benefit of their agriculture.

196

In the south – for example at Chancay – we see how the pottery forms change under Inca influence: thus we find jars of aryballoid shape with long thin necks. The black colouring and the incised designs become general, as in the Chimú-Inca style in the north. We find the same thing at Pukara, where forms derived from the aryballus also occur. The aryballi of Nazca and Puno are of exceptional beauty and magnificently painted – showing clearly that they were not produced locally.

The system of *mitimaes* (forced migrations) was an instrument of political and locial policy. This drastic method was used to uproot whole populations and trans-ser them from the more populous parts of the country to the areas where their fabour was required. In this way each region was made to produce the maximum yield of which it was capable.

Although the *mamacunas* lived in Cuzco, it is not here but in the coastal area that the finest woven fabrics have been discovered. Two examples of the sleeve-less tunics typical of Inca work may be quoted. One of these – a plain rectangle with two openings for the arms – is splendidly coloured, with a light pastel blue ground, three pink bands decorated with anthropomorphic figures and llamas, and a beige band decorated with abstract patterns in light red, cream and blue. In the second example – also rectangular in shape – the main pattern consists of vertical lines crossed by two parallel lines. The colours used are yellow, red and green, the single red lines being contrasted with two blue lines. The neck, the arm openings, the hem and the seam down the side are picked out with a multi-coloured braid. These two pieces are the finest specimens of Inca work I have seen.

The materials used in textile production were alpaca and vicuña wool and cotton. They were a State monopoly, supplies being issued to the people in accordance with prescribed rules.

In discussing Inca textiles we cannot rely on the evidence of Huaman Poma's drawings. These are often defective, and in any case do not show the full range of fabrics produced.

The men of the Inca empire wore a tunic coming down to their knees and a cloak which covered their shoulders and arms. It is surprising not to find any *ponchos*. The warriors also wore a tunic reaching to their knees, or sometimes shorter. They wore straps like puttees round their calves and knees, sandals on their feet and fillets *(llautus)* on their head. Women's clothes were longer, falling to their ankles. They wore many-coloured ribbons round their waists, and fastened their cloak on their shoulders with a fibula. People of high rank were distinguished by the bright colouring of their skirt, their tunic or their cloak. The Incas themselves wore breeches coming down to the knee. Men of the lower classes wore nothing but a loincloth.

There were highly skilled craftsmen in wood, who produced *keros* decorated with incised patterns and sometimes painted with water-resistant polychrome decoration, of the type now known as "Peruvian lacquer". These *keros* are the finest pieces we have in this style. Some of these beakers have handles in the form of a lizard or a feline. There are also stemmed cups, representations of *pacchas*, small vessels with two ears, puma heads, carved wooden armadillos, human heads, vessels supported by the figure of a man, others borne on the shoulders of two seated men. All of these are covered with splendid polychrome decoration – scenes of daily life, hunting scenes, battles, religious rites, festivals. Although this is essentially a primitive form of art these vessels acquire beauty and colour from their decoration, with its groups of figures and its flower ornaments – the *cantura*, the royal *ñucto* and other flowers of the mountain areas of Peru. This Peruvian lacquer and the vessels to which it is applied are a style typical of the Inca empire – though wooden *keros* with incised designs, but with no colouring, have also been found in Chimú territory. *(Plates 72, 73)*

In virtue of their Andean origin the Quechuas were masters of the art of carving stone, though the only examples of their art are large anthropomorphic or zoomorphic figures like those of Huari or Tiahuanaco. We find rudimentary mortars, semicircular in shape and with rounded sides, which have usually been hewn from a round block of stone; large mortars with four handles, stones of various shapes with a hole bored through the middle, axes, mortars with a plain base, stones with a circular orifice, mortars with a shallow cup, beautifully formed globular vessels, mortars with handles, and mortars with a rectangular or rounded base. The finely carved *conopas* (small idols) are beautifully stylised figures of the alpaca or containers in the form of human heads which held the ingredients designed to increase the fertility of cattle.

The stone maces are of high artistic quality, though they do not reach the same standard as the Mochica maces. They were of course intended for military rather than ceremonial use.

The Quechuas were also skilled in engraving on bone and in basketwork.

As already noted, we find various types of architecture at Cuzco, undoubtedly belonging to a number of different periods. I do not believe that the differences of style can be explained by the different techniques required for different types of building at the same period. The walls of Sacsahuamán show incredible architectural skill: we cannot conceive how stones weighing hundreds of tons can have been transported, fitted together and polished with as much care as the lens of a telescope. At a later period smaller stones were used, so carefully fitted together that we cannot insert a needle between them: we find this technique, for example, in the polygonal walls of Hatunrumiyoc, several buildings in Cuzco and the ruins of Putuhuasi. At Ollantaytambo and in the upper part of Machu Picchu we find walls of large rectangular blocks separated by very thin flakes of stone, belonging to the same period or to a period intermediate between Sacsahuamán and the polygonal type. Then there are the large buildings like the Coricancha and the Sillustani built in slightly convex blocks. And finally, during the period of Inca expansion, another new technique is developed, using carefully dressed stones with a polished external surface which are laid in the same fashion as adobe bricks: this technique is found at Pachacamac and in the latest buildings at Cuzco, Huánuco, Cajamarca and elsewhere in Peru. Houses were also built of uncut field stones set in clay, now called *pircas;* and in the north the blocks were fitted together with the help of smaller stones known as *paichillas.* In Inca architecture it was the weight of the blocks and the skill with which they were fitted together that gave the walls their massive strength.

It is easy to distinguish the different types of Inca buildings – the strongly built military installations situated in strategic positions, the great palaces, the huge temples, and the ordinary buildings in which the large populations of the cities were housed.

The Inca architects laid out their cities with great skill within the protective ramparts, seeking always the simplicity of straight lines. The remains of Cuzco, of Tambo Machay and of Ollontaytambo are splendid examples of their town planning. One of the most magnificent achievements of Inca architecture, however, is Machu Picchu, the eagles' eyrie perched on a remote peak above yawning abysses, a site without equal in the world for its impregnable strength and the splendour of the surrounding landscape. The visitor who reaches this lofty summit and contemplates the luxuriant vegetation of the forests around him is overwhelmed by the dynamic power of nature, which here reigns supreme. Machu Picchu achieves an extraordinary harmony between the beauty of the landscape and the creative genius of the men of the Inca period, whose technical achievements still amaze and puzzle us today.

The Quechuas were highly skilled agricultural and hydraulic engineers who practised terraced cultivation with great competence, showing a scientific genius equal to that of those who in more modern times have applied mathematics to the exploitation of the natural resources of the soil. They built suspension bridges, too, to reduce distances by road and speed up the movements of their armies. *(Plates 150-165)*

The people of Cuzco gave expression to their conception of eternity in the building known as the Coricancha. It was constructed in stone on a plan different from that of any other building in Cuzco, and its internal walls were faced with plaques of gold. The image of the sun, represented by a great disc of solid gold, occupied the place of honour in the innermost sanctuary. At certain hours of the day the rays of the sun shone directly on the disc, producing a magical effect which must have made a great impression on the faithful. According to Father Cobo their religion recognised a whole hierarchy of deities. The first place was occupied by Viracocha, the creator of the world, and after him came the sun, Apu Inti; the third place belonged to the god of thunder and lightning, whose name in Quechua was Illapa; then came the moon, Quilla; and finally, in fifth, sixth and seventh places, the stars, the sea and the earth.

I believe that Viracocha was the one god from whom the Incas could never break loose, though they sought to instruct the conquered peoples in the knowledge of new gods and new dogmas. The cult of Viracocha was deeply rooted in the culture of Peru and for two thousand years remained at the core of all Peruvian religious beliefs. In my view Viracocha is to be identified with the anthropomorphic feline god of all the peoples of ancient Peru. The Incas did not dare to displace him or to deprive him of his position as creator of the world and Supreme Being of the universe: accordingly they put the sun and all the other new divinities on a lower level. They themselves claimed to be descended from the sun and not from Viracocha, who was the father of all created things.

The chroniclers did their best to adjust some of the features of their own religion – the attributes of the saints and so on – to the religious ideas of the Peruvians.

140, 141 →

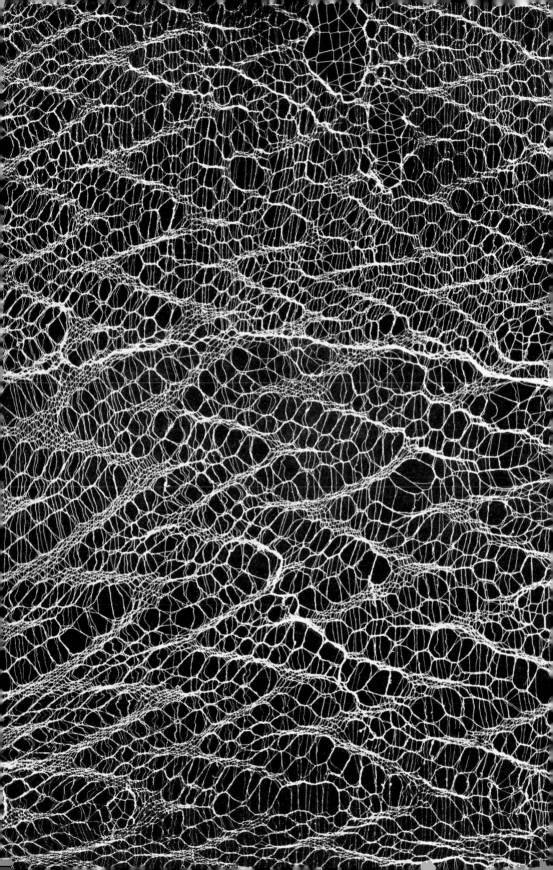

142

143

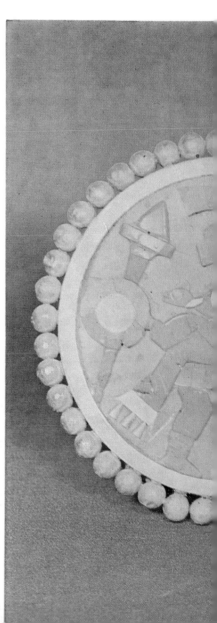

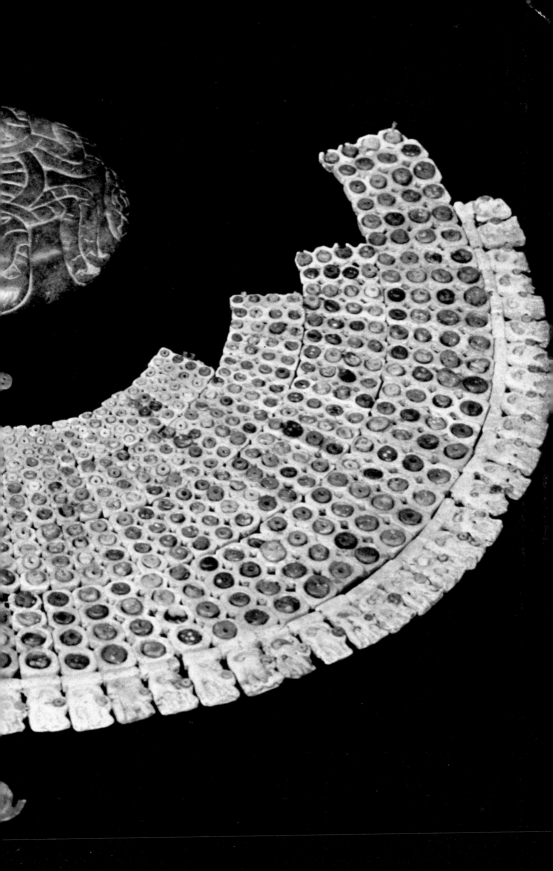

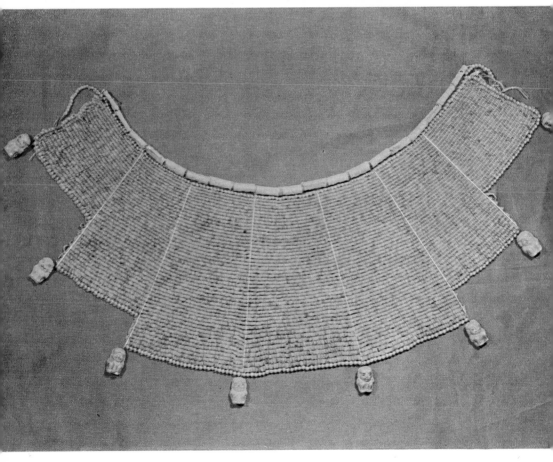

150

151

152–163 →

164   166, 167→

165

It was Viracocha who gave the sun the power to create food. The moon was the sun's wife and the stars were their children. Viracocha was supposed to be invisible, and in his temple he was represented by a kind of bundle of cloths. The moon was thought of in the form of a woman.

The Incas worshipped the sun as their principal deity, and it was from him that their dynasty was supposed to descend. The sun was represented by a gold disc or by a human figure, also made of gold. The belly of the idol was filled with gold dust mingled with the ashes of the hearts of the Inca emperors.

We know that the great god Pachacamac had his temple in the town of the same name; and this god too was none other than Viracocha himself. The idol found in this temple represented the anthropomorphic feline deity. The temple was a Mecca to all the inhabitants of the coastal area. The worshippers offered to the god a liquor made with *quinua*, maize or *molle;* guineapigs were sacrificed, and on great occasions llamas. Even after the Spanish conquest offerings continued to be made to the god, in the form of silver coins which were beaten to efface the royal arms and anointed with blood and *chicha.*

Coca and many other plants used today by herbalists served as offerings in the pre-Hispanic period. The *villac-umu* (a term which Cobo translates as "diviner" or "sorcerer") and the *huillacac-umuc* or high priest no doubt took part in magic practices as well as religious rites, designed to impress the people with the importance of their role as priests and direct spiritual advisers to the Emperor. At this period, too, there were oracles, like those of Huanacauri and Pachacamac.

There were many predictions looking forward to the arrival of bearded strangers who should conquer the native peoples. The famous diviner Chalco, consulted by Huayna Capac when an eagle appeared in the sky pursued by falcons, prophesied wars, the spilling of the royal blood, and the decline of the Empire – and this at a time when the Empire of the Incas was at the height of its splendour. The Emperors had a whole series of palaces in Cuzco, the walls of the temples were clad with plaques of gold, there were artificial gardens planted with plants made of gold. The Inca armies had conquered an immense territory extending from the north of Ecuador to the middle of Chile, with a total length of some 3,000 miles and an area of 350,000 square miles.

The Incas can undoubtedly be reckoned among the greatest conquerors known to history. They were driven to these conquests by overweening ambition, the urge to dominate ever vaster territories, a thirst for power, the dream of greatness. There was no social or economic reason, no threat of absorption by other peoples. The Inca Empire expanded purely out of a desire for power and glory, with no thought other than that of imposing its will on other peoples. The children of the great nobles and dignitaries of the conquered peoples were sent to Cuzco as hostages and to be indoctrinated.

In the panorama of world history the Incas can be compared with conquerors like Philip of Macedon and Alexander the Great. And as with other conquerors it was/ when they were in the full pride of their conquests and enjoying a glory equal (in Mason's words) to that of Genghis Khan, Alexander or Napoleon, that the oracles and the revelations granted in the temples – soon to be followed by first-hand reports – announced the arrival of strange bearded men who had set out in conquest of the vast possessions of the Incas. These invaders of unknown origin spread terror wherever they went with their horses, which were quite new to the inhabitants of the Empire, and their firearms which were also quite un-known. To the natives all this was the work of demons. And so began the destruction of what little remained of the native cultures.

The invasion meant the beginning of the end for all the small cultures which for thousands of years had sought in the world as it was then known the elements they needed to solve their problems and create the characteristic civilisations of Peru, had shown a lively capacity for invention, and had splendidly achieved distinctive personalities of their own and their own individual artistic styles. These cultures had run through the whole cycle of development, from birth to decline. Twice they had fallen under the sway of conquerors who had seized the whole territory of Peru and had had to accept the fate of the vanquished. But this troubled history made possible the creation of the kingdoms and empires which may not have left us much evidence of their artistic talent but did at any rate demonstrate another facet of the native genius, particularly in the ruling caste – their capacity to organise a great empire and achieve a political structure based on ideas greatly in advance of their period.

The Spanish Conquest
With the arrival of the Spaniards the artistic inspiration of the peoples of Tahuan-tisuvo was extinguished. It was as if an earthquake shock had utterly overthrown

the structure built up over the years. The few traces of creative art which sur-vived under the Empire as a glorious heritage from the peoples of the Florescent Epoch now disappeared for good.

Scattered throughout Peru we find a few terracotta jars with a green and brown glaze, the meagre contribution made by Hispanic art to the pottery of Peru. These jars are found as grave goods, almost invariably associated with looms, weaving implements, baskets containing balls of thread, spindles, combs and other objects. In Cuzco we found vessels representing a *plaza de toros*, an African lion, drinking vessels with three concentric parts for three different liquids, negroid types, sirens playing the guitar, dragons with curling tails, and some stone objects – reminders of what the Peruvian cultures of the past had achieved.

Even when the Spaniards had occupied the whole of Peru and consolidated their hold on the country they were unable to eradicate the cult of the dead to which the Indians attached so much importance. The tradition continued; but now the dead who had once been adorned with splendid necklaces of turquoise, lapis lazuli and gold had to be content with cheap glass trinkets from Venice, imported by the Spaniards and profitably exchanged for precious metals.

The textiles were now of extremely poor quality. The fine moulded and painted pottery of earlier times was replaced by coarse pots decorated with crude patterns in relief. The representations of the feline god disappeared and the Cross took their place. The spiritual cataclysm which had destroyed the native cultures left the Peruvians no other resource than to embrace a different creed. Their god – the humanised feline, Viracocha, the Sun – had forsaken them, and the ancient cultures of Peru were condemned to die.

In this desolate spiritual landscape, while the native peoples were being thrown into slavery and their arts were in decay, the only ray of light in their darkness and distress was the promise held out to them by Christ and His Church.

SYNOPTIC CHRONOLOGICAL TABLE

In order to present a complete picture of the cultures of Peru, fitting each one into its place within the different epochs and periods, I have selected for consideration the principal valleys of the coastal area and the most important cultural centres in the highlands during the prehistoric period.

I divide the coastal valleys into three groups – northern, central and southern:

Northern: Piura, Lambayeque, Pacasmayo, Chicama, Santa Catalina, Virú, Chao, Santa, Nepeña, Casma and Huarmey.

Central: Supe, Huacho, Chancay and Lima.

Southern: Cañete, Chincha, Ica, Nazca and Palpa.

I regard the following as the most important centres in the highland area:

Northern: Chota, Cajamarca and Huamachuco.

Central: Ayacucho.

Southern: Arequipa, Cuzco and Puno.

This is the framework of the synoptic chronological table which follows. In it I have classified the various cultures systematically on the basis of the characteristic features found on each site.

One further remark. It has not been possible to mention in the table the discoveries of pre-Cupisnique material at Lauricocha and Toquepala, since it is not practicable to include a separate column for Huánuco and Moquegua.

I believe that the Early Ceramic Epoch must have lasted for a considerable time, for it extends from the Queneto culture to the pre-Cupisnique phase and the other peoples of this epoch.

The pre-Cupisnique and "Old Guañape" pottery clearly indicate the beginnings of a culture, but show also that there had been a definite advance over a long period before the birth of this culture. For this reason I date the Early Ceramic Epoch between 2000 and 1250 B.C., corresponding to the pre-Cupisnique and Old Guañape phases, and probably to the beginnings of Vicus.

The following table is based not only on a study of the development of the various cultures at different times but on the dates obtained by radiocarbon dating. Most of the dates given agree with the dates shown in the tables by Mason and other archaeologists and with the radiocarbon datings given by Junius Bird.
The dates are as follows:

Pre-Ceramic Epoch	8000 to 2000 B.C.
Early Ceramic Epoch	2000 to 1250 B.C.
Formative Epoch	1250 B.C. to 1
Florescent Epoch	A.D. 1 to 800
Epoch of Fusion	A.D. 800 to 1300
Imperial Epoch	A.D. 1300 to 1532
Conquest	A.D. 1532

I CULTURES OF THE NORTHERN COASTAL AREA

II CULTURES OF THE CENTRAL COASTAL AREA

III CULTURES OF THE SOUTHERN COASTAL AREA

IV CULTURES OF THE HIGHLAND AREA

SELECT BIBLIOGRAPHY

Other Works by Señor Rafael Larco Hoyle

LOS MOCHICAS (The Mochicas), Vol. 1 (Chapter 1, Origin and developpent of social groups on the coast of Peru. Chapter 2, Geography). Lima, Peru, 1938.

LOS MOCHICAS, Vol. 2 (Chapters 3-6, Race, language, writing, system of government). Lima, Peru, 1940.

LOS CUPISNIQUES (The Cupisniques). (A study presented at the 27th meeting of the International Congress of Americanists in Lima). Lima, Peru, 1941.

LA ESCRITURA MOCHICA SOPRA PALLARES (Mochica writing on beans). From the *Revista Geográfica Americana*. Buenos Aires, Argentina, 1942.

LA ESCRITURA PERUANA SOPRA PALLARES (Peruvian writing on beans). From the *Revista Geográfica Americana*. Buenos Aires, Argentina, 1943.

LA CULTURA SALINAR (The Salinar culture). Buenos Aires, Argentina, 1944.

LA ESCRITURA PERUANA SOPRA PALLARES. Published by the Sociedad Argentina de Antropología. Buenos Aires, Argentina, 1944.

LA ESCRITURA PERUANA PRE-INCANA (Pre-Inca writing in Peru). From the journal *El México Antiguo*. Mexico City, 1944.

LA CULTURA VIRÚ (The Virú culture). Buenos Aires, Argentina, 1945.

LOS MOCHICAS (Uhle's Pre-Chimú and Kroeber's Early Chimú). Buenos Aires, Argentina, 1945.

A CULTURE SEQUENCE FOR THE NORTH COAST OF PERU. In *Handbook of South American Indians*, Washington D.C., 1946.

LOS CUPISNIQUES. Buenos Aires, Argentinia, 1945.

CRONOLOGÍA ARQUEOLÓGICA DEL NORTE DEL PERÚ (The archaeological chronology of northern Peru). Buenos Aires, Argentina, 1948.

LA CULTURA SANTA (The Santa culture). 1962.

LA DIVINIDAD FELINICA LAMBAYEQUE (The feline deity of Lambayeque). 1962.

LAS EPOCAS PERUANAS (The epochs of Peruvian history). 1963.

LA CULTURA VICUS (The Vicus culture). 1965.

MUSEO RAFAEL LARCO HERRERA (The Rafael Larco Herrera Museum). 1965.

CHECAN. Nagel, Geneva, 1965.

LIST OF ILLUSTRATIONS

(Unless otherwise indicated, the objects illustrated are in the Rafael Larco Herrera Museum, Lima).

24 *Formative Epoch. Virú. Stylised condor. Jar with negative decoration.*

25 *Formative Epoch. Orange ware. Portrait head.*

26 *Formative Epoch. Salinar. Bottle-shaped jar with incised decoration, painted white with red areas.*

27 *Formative Epoch. Virú. Stylised head of feline.*

28 *Formative Epoch. Salinar. Stirrup-spouted jar representing a monkey.*

29 *Formative Epoch. Salinar. Jar representing a feline.*

30 *Epoch of Fusion. Central Huari. Parrot.*

31 *Florescent Epoch. Mochica IV. Portrait of a high dignitary. Black pottery, originally inlaid with mother-of-pearl and turquoise.*

32 *Florescent Epoch. Mochica II. High dignitary, seated.*

33 *Florescent Epoch. Mochica I. High dignitary, seated. Black pottery, originally inlaid with turquoise.*

34 *Florescent Epoch. Mochica IV. The supreme penalty: the victim's face has been flayed, he is tied to a tree and is being devoured by birds of prey.*

35 *Florescent Epoch. Mochica IV. High military leader dispensing justice.*

36 *Florescent Epoch. Mochica IV. Symbolic representation of a high dignitary.*

37 *Florescent Epoch. Mochica IV. Sculptural representation of a* chasqui *with his pouch.*

38 *Florescent Epoch. Mochica IV. Kneeling warrior, wearing large necklace and nose ornament.*

39 *Florescent Epoch. Mochica IV. Military leader kneeling, with a mace in his hand.*

40 *Florescent Epoch. Mochica IV. Panoply of arms in humanised form, symbolising a warrior.*

41 Ibid *(detail).*

42 *Florescent Epoch. Mochica IV. High dignitary who has suffered amputation of the nose and part of the lip.*

43 *Florescent Epoch. Mochica III. Anthropomorphic stag taken captive.*

44 *Florescent Epoch. Mochica IV. Messenger idealised in the form of an anthropomorphic stag.*

45 *Florescent Epoch. Mochica II. The god Aia Paec.*

46 *Florescent Epoch. Mochica IV. Vessel with pictorial scene which gave the clue to the decipherment of the Mochica ideographic script.*

47 *Florescent Epoch. Mochica IV. A fine pictorial scene representing a battle, with the leaders directing operations.*

48 *Florescent Epoch. Mochica IV. Jar with painted decoration. After the battle the vanquished, stripped naked, carry a chief, also naked, in a litter.*

49 *Florescent Epoch. Mochica IV. The deity on a balsa raft shaped like a fish, with a woman prisoner.*

50 *Florescent Epoch. The feline deity with many feline heads on his face.*

51 *Florescent Epoch. Mochica IV. Sculptured jar on a religious theme, representing an anthropomorphic idol in the coils of the two-headed snake which symbolises the rainbow.*

52 *Florescent Epoch. Mochica IV. Caudal appendage of copper – an ornament worn by Mochica warriors. From Vicus. (Private collection).*

53 *Florescent Epoch. Mochica IV. The deity flying on a bird's back.*

54–56 *Florescent Epoch. Mochica IV (54) and Mochica III (55–56). Agricultural deity, half toad and half jaguar, symbolising the union of water, land, and the fruits of the earth. In some representations manioc sprouts from his body.*

57 *Florescent Epoch. Mochica III. Jaguar.*

58 *Florescent Epoch. Mochica II. Llama.*

59 *Florescent Epoch. Mochica IV. Monkeys gathering heads of maize. Detail from No. 60.*

60 *Florescent Epoch. Mochica IV. Bottle-shaped jar decorated with reliefs. Aia Paec stripping maize in presence of the agricultural deity, with monkeys gathering the grain.*

61 *Florescent Epoch. Mochica IV. Bowl decorated with reliefs. The deity on his balsa raft, with cormorants helping him with his fishing.*

62 *Florescent Epoch. Mochica IV. Jar in the shape of a potato.*

63 *Florescent Epoch. Mochica III. Jar in the shape of an anthropomorphic potato.*

64 *Imperial Epoch. Chancay. Anthropomorphic double jar.*

65 *Florescent Epoch. Mochica V. Two monkeys clinging together.*

66 *Imperial Epoch. Chimú-Inca. Jar representing a roe-deer's head.*

67 *Florescent Epoch. Mochica III. Jar representing a type of crab found on the coasts of Peru.*

68 *Florescent Epoch. Mochica IV. Puma.*

69 *Florescent Epoch. Mochica IV. Cormorant.*

70 *Florescent Epoch. Lambayeque. Red spout-and-bridge jar.*

71 *Florescent Epoch. Lambayeque. Zapote fruits. Jar with double spout and bridge.*

72 *Imperial Epoch. Inca. Pottery* kero.

73 *Imperial Epoch. Inca. Painted wooden* kero *decorated with figures, including a warrior armed with a shield. From Cuzco. (Museum of Ethnography, Geneva).*

74 *Epoch of Fusion. Huari-Lambayeque. Semi-rectangular head-shaped jar with spout and bridge.*

75 *Florescent Epoch. Santa. Man with llama.*

76 *Imperial Epoch. Chancay. Zoomorphic jar.*

77 *Imperial Epoch. Chimú. Peruvian dog, hairless, with the typical warts.*

78 *Imperial Epoch. Chancay. Zoomorphic double jar with spout and bridge.*

79 *Florescent Epoch. Santa. High dignitary seated on a throne, with four men holding a cloak over his head to form a canopy.*

80 *Florescent Epoch. Nazca A. Fisherman.*

81 *Florescent Epoch. Nazca A. Semi-anthropomorphic sperm whale.*

82 *Florescent Epoch. Nazca B. Double spout-and-bridge jar with the ornament typical of this period of decadence.*

83 *Florescent Epoch. Chanca A. Jar representing a woman.*

84 *Florescent Epoch. Nazca B. Cylindrical jar.*

85 *Florescent Epoch. Nazca B. Double spout-and-bridge jar representing a basket of fruit.*

86 *Epoch of Fusion. Rukana. Bird. A very rare example with stirrup spout, not normally found in the southern area.*

87 *Epoch of Fusion. South Huari A. Double vessel with a zoomorphic figure in the centre, showing Chanca influence.*

88 *Epoch of Fusion. South Huari A. Anthropomorphic double jar with spout and bridge, painted in polychrome.*

89 *Florescent Epoch. Santa. Warrior on the roof of a house, attended by women, with other women on the lower floor. (Private collection).*

90 *Florescent Epoch. Nazca B. Globular anthropomorphic vessel, with representations of the feline.*

91 *Florescent Epoch. Mochica IV. Jar of gilded copper, used to hold the lime which was mixed with the coca leaves for chewing.*

92 *Imperial Epoch. Chimú. Ceremonial vessel with a feline carved from wood inlaid with the teeth of sperm whales and mother-of-pearl, and the bowl in the form of a gourd.*

93 *Florescent Epoch. Mochica. Small masks of gilded copper.*

94 *Imperial Epoch. Chimú. Head of sceptre, cast by the* cire perdue *method, representing a ceremonial scene.*

95 *Formative Epoch. Pacopampa. Mortar of phonolite (clinkstone) with deep incised ornament.*

96 *Florescent Epoch. Mochica. Head of sceptre in wood.*

97 *Formative Epoch. Cupisnique. One of the few known full-length sculptures of the human body in stone.*

98 *Imperial Epoch. Chimú. Idol of carob-wood, originally covered with gold and silver.*

99–100 *Formative Epoch. Pacopampa. Stone mortars and pestles. The mortars represent the condor deity and the feline deity. The pestles end in snakes' heads.*

101 *Florescent Epoch. Mochica. Handle of spear-thrower carved from stag's horn, representing a feline head.*

102 *Imperial Epoch. Chimú. Head of sceptre.*

103 *Formative Epoch. Virú. Mace decorated with two owls' heads.*

104 *Imperial Epoch. Chimú-Inca. Jar in the form of a fruit. (Private collection).*

105 *Florescent Epoch. Mochica IV. Seated warrior. (Private collection).*

106 *Florescent Epoch. Huari. A fine polychrome jar in which the modelling and the painting are perfectly harmonised. (Private collection).*

107 *Epoch of Fusion. North Huari B. Anthropomorphic feline deity. Mochica work showing Huari influence.*

108 *Florescent Epoch. Nazca A. Anthropomorphic feline deity holding fruit. (Private collection).*

109 *Formative Epoch. Paracas Cavernas. Anthropomorphic jar. (Private collection).*

110 *Florescent Epoch. Previously called Recuay. Warrior. (Private collection).*

111 *Florescent Epoch. Nazca. Fisherman. A rare example of a polychrome jar with incised decoration. (Private collection).*

112 *Formative Epoch. Orange-ware jar representing a bird. (Private collection).*

113 *Imperial Epoch. Chancay. Painted jar decorated with a cormorant. (Private collection).*

114 *Florescent Epoch. Mochica. Four people collecting snails from cacti for food. (National Museum, Lima).*

115 *Florescent Epoch. Nazca. Bird. A rare example of a polychrome jar with incised decoration. (Private collection).*

116 *Florescent Epoch. Huari. A fine jar representing a man carrying two pots. (Private collection).*

117 *Formative Epoch. Vicus. Anthropomorphic jar. (Private collection).*

118 *Florescent Epoch. Chanca. Jar with double spout and bridge, in stepped rectangular form. One of the finest Chanca jars known.*

119 *Imperial Epoch. Chancay. Jar in the shape of a bird. (Private collection).*

120 *Imperial Epoch. Chimú. Copper medallions, perhaps originally gilded, showing remarkably fine workmanship.*

121   Ibid.

122   *Imperial Epoch. Chimú. Silver ear-plugs with delicate openwork ornament. The finest specimens of Chimú jewellery known.*

123   *Florescent Epoch. Huari. Six small turquoise idols. An owl carved from slate.*

124   *Found at Vicus. Maces and axes. It is not known what pottery these were associated with.*

125   *Fragment of cloth from the southern coastal area of Peru.*

126   *Imperial Epoch. Chimú. The only specimen known of the gold ornaments worn by a high Chimú dignitary. They consist of a breastplate with two shoulder pieces, ear-plugs, a necklace, a bracelet and a crown with gold plumes.*

127   *Florescent Epoch. Lambayeque. Three large gold jars, ranging from 850 to 1200 grammes (30 to 42 ounces) in weight, representing the head of the feline deity.*

128   *Florescent Epoch. Nazca. Fragment of cloth.*

129   *Florescent Epoch. Mochica IV. Vessel decorated with a boat which, when the vessel is full, seems to be floating on the surface of the liquid. (Private collection).*

130   *Formative Epoch. Vicus. Jars in the form of human heads. (Private collection).*

131   *Florescent Epoch. Chanca A. Figurine representing a naked woman. (Private collection).*

132   *Formative Epoch. Vicus. Negative decorated jar representing a swimmer supporting himself on an inflated skin. (Private collection).*

133   *Florescent Epoch. Mochica. Fragment of cloth found in the Santa valley.*

134   *Found at Vicus. Heads of maces with openwork decoration. It is not known what pottery these were associated with. (Private collection).*

135–138   *Vicus. Knives. Association with pottery not known. (Private collection).*

139   *Formative Epoch and Florescent Epoch. Cupisnique and Mochica IV. Necklaces of turquoise and gold. Pendants in turquoise and onyx. The necklace in the centre is in rock crystal.*

All photographs in this volume are by GÉRARD BERTIN, GENEVA except Nos. 73 and 143 (Jean Arlaud, Geneva) and Nos. 148, 149, 166 and 166 (Rafael Larco Herrera Museum, Lima).

INDEX

Imprimé en Suisse   Printed in Switzerland

THE TEXT AND ILLUSTRATIONS
IN THIS VOLUME WERE PRINTED
ON THE PRESSES OF NAGEL
PUBLISHERS IN GENEVA.

PLATES ENGRAVED BY CLICHÉS UNION, PARIS

PRINTED IN SWITZERLAND

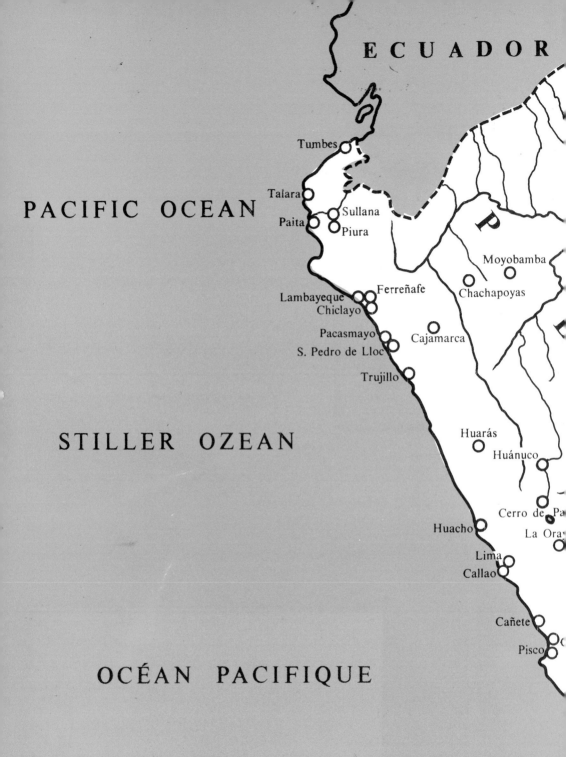

ECUADOR

PACIFIC OCEAN

STILLER OZEAN

OCÉAN PACIFIQUE

Tumbes

Talara
Sullana
Paita
Piura

Moyobamba

Lambayeque
Ferreñafe
Chiclayo
Chachapoyas

Pacasmayo
S. Pedro de Lloc
Cajamarca

Trujillo

Huarás
Huánuco

Cerro de Pa
La Ora
Huacho

Lima
Callao

Cañete
Pisco